PENGUIN CLASSICS

UTOPIA

ADVISORY EDITOR: BETTY RADICE

SIR THOMAS MORE also SAINT THOMAS MORE, was born in London in 1478. He was a page in the household of Archbishop Morton, who sent him to Oxford, and was called to the bar, where he was eminently successful. He became an MP and Undersheriff of London, and while envoy to Flanders began writing *Utopia* in Latin, finishing it in 1516. He was appointed privy councillor of Henry VIII in 1518 and, recommended by Wolsey, was elected Speaker of the House of Commons in 1525. On the fall of Wolsey he succeeded against his will as Lord Chancellor of England, the first layman to hold the office. He came into conflict with the king by refusing to acknowledge the sovereign as sole head of the church, and in 1532 he resigned. Charged with high treason, he steadfastly refused to take an oath impugning the pope's authority or upholding Henry VIII's divorce from Catherine of Aragon. During his imprisonment he prepared a *Dialogue of Comfort Against Tribulation*. He was beheaded in 1535; his canonization occurred four hundred years later.

A friend of Erasmus, Colet and Lyly and pupil of Linacre and Grocyn, More was internationally admired and respected as a man and a scholar. He was author also of the *Life of John Picus, Earl of Mirandula* and of the *History of Richard III*.

PAUL TURNER was born in 1917, and educated at Winchester and King's College, Cambridge, He served in the RNVR (air branch) during the war, and then taught English literature at London, Cambridge and Ankara Universities, before joining the Oxford English Faculty in 1964. He is now an Emeritus Fellow of Linacre College, Oxford, and has recently published a volume on the Victorians in the *Oxford History of English Literature*. His translations from Greek, Latin and German include Longus's *Daphnis and Chloe*, Lucian's *Satirical Sketches*, Ovid's *Art of Love*, Hoffman's *The King's Bride* and Fouqué's *Undine*.

THOMAS MORE

UTOPIA

TRANSLATED
WITH AN INTRODUCTION BY
PAUL TURNER

PENGUIN BOOKS

PENGUIN BOOKS

Published by the Penguin Group
Penguin Books Ltd, 27 Wrights Lane, London W8 5TZ, England
Penguin Books USA Inc., 375 Hudson Street, New York, New York 10014, USA
Penguin Books Australia Ltd, Ringwood, Victoria, Australia
Penguin Books Canada Ltd, 10 Alcorn Avenue, Toronto, Ontario, Canada M4V 3B2
Penguin Books (NZ) Ltd, 182–190 Wairau Road, Auckland 10, New Zealand

Penguin Books Ltd, Registered Offices: Harmondsworth, Middlesex, England

This translation first published 1965
40

Printed in England by Clays Ltd, St Ives plc
Set in Monotype Garamond

CONTENTS

INTRODUCTION

1

THE position of More's *Utopia* is rather like that of the baby in
the Judgment of Solomon. One school of thought claims it as a
Catholic tract, in which anything resembling communist propa-
ganda should be interpreted as moral allegory. Another claims
it as a political manifesto, in which all references to religion
should be firmly ignored. Both claimants seem more concerned
with the rights of ownership than with the work itself, and are
quite prepared to chop it in half, or at least to pluck out and
cast from them any part of its anatomy that offends them.

A translator is at best a sort of foster-mother; but perhaps
the process of translation tends to generate more quasi-
maternal feeling for a book than the process of criticism – for
I really do not care which school *Utopia* belongs to, so long as
justice is done to its artistic vitality. To my mind, the most
important questions to be asked about it are, what kind of book
is it, and what does it say?

2

What kind of book? We can start with the description given on
the title page of the first edition (1516), a delightfully slim
quarto of 110 pages. There it is 'a really splendid little book, as
entertaining as it is instructive'. In other words it professes,
like Horace's *Satires*, to 'tell the truth with a laugh', or, like
Lucian's *True History*, 'not merely to be witty and entertaining,
but also to say something interesting'. We know from Erasmus
that More was particularly fond of Lucian, and the two friends
translated some of his works into Latin in about 1505. Among
the four pieces done by More was the dialogue which appears
in the Penguin Classics Lucian under the title, *Menippus goes to
Hell* (pp. 97–110). This probably suggested the literary form
of *Utopia*, a familiar conversation raising a serious problem,

followed by a fantastic traveller's tale describing an imaginary place in which the problem is solved.

Lucian's traveller is the Cynic philosopher, Menippus; More's is a student of philosophy called Raphael Hythlodaeus. *Raphael* is Hebrew for 'God has healed', and in the Apocryphal *Book of Tobit* the Archangel Raphael guides Tobias on a journey, which ends with the curing of Tobit's blindness, and the recovery of his property. So the name is quite appropriate for a character who tries to open people's eyes to the causes of social evils, and the sources of prosperity. But most of the proper names in *Utopia* (as in Lucian's *True History*) are of the *Hythlodaeus* type; that is, they are words of Greek derivation, specially invented for the purpose, and designed to be immediately intelligible. Thus *Hythlodaeus* means 'dispenser of nonsense', *Utopia* means 'not place', *Anydrus* (the name of a river) means 'not water', and *Ademus* (the title of a chief magistrate) means 'not people'. It is clear from an ironical passage in a letter to Peter Gilles (*The Correspondence of Sir Thomas More*, Princeton, 1947, p. 91) that More expected the educated reader to understand these names; and to ensure that their significance was not overlooked, he mentioned in the book itself that the Utopian language 'contains some traces of Greek in place-names and official titles' (p. 100). As modern education very seldom includes Greek, I thought the only way of implementing More's intention was to convert such proper names into English equivalents. Accordingly, *Hythlodaeus* (who comes from Portugal) appears as Nonsenso, *Anydrus* as Nowater, and *Ademus* as Nopeople. *Utopia*, however, seems too well known to be changed, so this name is retained, along with its derivatives, *Utopian* and *Utopos* or *Utopus*; but its meaning (Noplace) should be borne in mind throughout.

I make no apology for the slightly comic effect created by these equivalents, though it may come as a shock to those who picture More exclusively as a saint and martyr, or as a political thinker. Erasmus says that More had 'from earliest childhood such a passion for jokes, that one might almost suppose he had been born for them' (*Erasmi Epistolae*, IV, Oxford, 1922, p. 16). He even enjoyed jokes against himself. But in *Utopia* these names are not only meant to be funny; they are also meant to remind the reader that the places and people in question are purely imaginary. By their emphasis on nonsense and non-existence they imply something very like Lucian's warning in the Preface to the *True History*: 'Let this voluntary confession forestall any future criticism: I am writing about things entirely outside my own experience or anyone else's, things that have no reality whatever.' They enable him, like the 'all-licens'd fool' in *King Lear*, to tell home-truths with comparative safety – to be as serious as he likes, while retaining, for use in emergencies, the excuse that he is only clowning.

This emphasis on fantasy is paradoxically combined, as in modern science fiction, with an emphasis on realism. Raphael Nonsenso is introduced into a genuinely autobiographical passage describing More's visit to Flanders in 1515, and tells his story in the presence of Peter Gilles, who was in fact the Town Clerk of Antwerp. Similarly, Nonsenso's imaginary travels are grafted on to the historical voyages of Amerigo Vespucci, and the starting-point for the journey to Utopia is a fort at Cape Frio, in which Vespucci left twenty-four men in 1504. The pretence that the conversation with Nonsenso really took place is worked out in amusing detail, with the collaboration of Peter Gilles: if somebody had not coughed at precisely the wrong moment, the exact position of the island could have been inserted in the text, and a certain English clergyman could have achieved his ambition to become the first Bishop of Utopia.

There was once a fashion for publishing Do-It-Yourself detective stories, which provided the reader with cigarette-ends, hair-pins, and other three-dimensional clues in cellophane packets. In a similar attempt to offer first-hand evidence for the civilization described in the text, Peter Gilles appended the Utopian alphabet, and a specimen of Utopian poetry. The language is quite carefully constructed: one can, for instance, detect a logical system of inflexions for the first personal pronoun (nominative: *he*, accusative: *ha*, possessive: *heman*).

One function of these realistic devices is to amuse intelligent readers by hoaxing the unintelligent; and apparently some people were actually taken in. The publisher's introduction to More's Latin epigrams (1518) mentions 'a certain fathead' who said he did not see why More should be so much admired for his *Utopia*, since all he did was write down what somebody else had told him. This pretence of second-hand reporting may be regarded as another protective technique. Raphael Nonsenso is the only person who says anything unorthodox: More's own contributions to the conversation are usually quite conventional. The sole indication that Nonsenso may act as More's mouthpiece is the fact that in Utopian *he* means 'I'.

The form, then, of *Utopia* was designed not only to entertain, but also to create a context in which More could say what he liked, without laying himself open to too much criticism. It enabled him, in an age when rash expressions of opinion were apt to land one in the Tower, to disclaim responsibility for any view that might be considered subversive. This was quite in keeping with his apparent habit of dodging about behind a smoke-screen of humour: in one of his dialogues he makes someone say to him, 'Ye use to look so sadly [i.e. seriously] when ye mean merrily, that many times men doubt whether ye speak in sport, when ye mean good earnest' (*English Works*, 1557, p.127B). It was also not unlike the cautious avoidance of direct statement by which he tried, in the last year of his life, to minimize the danger of being 'The King's good servant, but God's first'.

3

Within the sanctuary of ambiguity constructed by its form, what does *Utopia* say? It begins by pointing out the irrational barbarity of capital punishment for theft, and argues that the only way to reduce the number of thieves is to reduce the number of people who must either steal or starve. In this connexion it attacks the conversion of arable land into pasture, and other contemporary practices liable to cause unemployment. It also suggests, as an alternative to hanging, a system of penal servitude. It then debates the question whether a sensible person should be willing to serve at Court, and satirizes the unscrupulous behaviour of the average king, especially his habit of starting aggressive wars, and his dishonest methods of raising money. Finally, it contrasts the unhappy state of

European society with conditions in an ideal country, where human life is organized in the best possible way.

With all of this except the last sentence most critics would probably agree; but many have found it impossible to believe that Utopia is really offered as a model of perfection, or that More is seriously recommending the Utopian way of life. It is not merely that the Utopians have some rather peculiar habits, such as using golden chamber-pots, and arranging for prospective brides and bridegrooms to inspect one another naked before committing themselves. These can, if necessary, be dismissed as jokes (though John Aubrey has a story[1] which suggests that the latter system was once put into practice, if somewhat unilaterally, in More's own household). The real difficulty arises from more important aspects of Utopian civilization. Can a devout Catholic, it is asked, have advocated such things as euthanasia, the marriage of priests, and divorce by mutual consent on grounds of incompatibility? Can a man who described himself on his own epitaph as 'troublesome to heretics', and wrote hundreds of pages against them, have recommended religious toleration? Can a large property-owner, whose income was once the equivalent of £8,000 a year at the present day, and who later compared the rich to the hen that laid the golden eggs, have been a crypto-communist?

The usual answer to these rhetorical questions is that Utopia does not represent a positive ideal, but a negative attack on European wickedness. Its object is to shame Christians into behaving not worse, as they do now, but far better than the poor Utopian heathen. In his *Introduction to Utopia* (London, 1945), which two later critics have rightly described as the best book of its kind available, Prof. H. W. Donner writes:

It was not the constitution of commonwealths that More desired to reform, but the spirit. The Utopian institutions can be nothing except 'very absurd' without the spirit that informs them. They must not be copied, but surpassed by Christian institutions. The community of goods that reason recommends to the Utopians must be excelled in the spiritual community of all Christians. . . . It is not our institutions that we must destroy, but those evil passions which are at the root of the abuses. More's programme of reform was one of personal amelioration. . . .

The *Utopia* does not attempt a final solution of the problems of human society – for More was too wise to attempt the impossible – but it contains an appeal addressed to all of us, which allows of no refusal, that we should try and do each one his share to mend our own selves and ease the burden of our fellow-men, to improve mankind and prepare for the life to come. (pp. 79–83)

Personally, I feel dissatisfied by such attempts to make the communism in *Utopia* metaphorical, and to water down all its social, economic, and political suggestions into a mere call for individual repentance. I am simple minded enough to believe, with certain qualifications, that the book means what it says, and that it *does* attempt to solve the problems of human society.

Of course, it does not offer a final solution. The Utopian prayer-book explicitly allows for the possibility of improvement: 'If I am wrong, and if some other ... social system would be better and more acceptable to Thee, I pray Thee in Thy goodness to let me know it' (p. 128). And, of course, if closely questioned, More would cheerfully admit that in certain matters Christian revelation *has* suggested improvements on Utopian practices and beliefs. But surely the whole emphasis of the book is on the rightness of Utopian institutions, not on their wrongness when judged by Christian standards.

We are still left with the problem of apparent contradictions (which I have discussed in the Notes and Appendix) between the views expressed in *Utopia* and in More's other works. Some of these contradictions are like the ghost in *Julius Caesar*: they vanish as soon as one tries to find out more about them. But when they survive investigation, I see no reason for doctoring a plain statement in one book, in order to make it square with what is said in another.

> Do I contradict myself?
> Very well then ... I contradict myself;
> I am large ... I contain multitudes.

Certainly More was quite unlike Whitman: he would never have thought inconsistency a sign of greatness. But he was equally unlike the type of person that he satirizes on page 75, who is 'ashamed to admit that his first idea might have been wrong'. It is much easier to imagine him praying, like a Utopian, to be shown where he was wrong, so that he could, if necessary, change his mind.

4

Let us assume, then, that Utopia is what it appears to be, a blue-print, however provisional, for a perfect society. Just how perfect would it be to live in? It offers the material benefits of a welfare state which provides every member of the community with food, clothing, housing, education, and medical treat-ment. Working hours are reasonably short, six hours a day – but this is achieved by limiting the supply of consumer-goods to the barest essentials. Result: heavy casualties among the minor pleasures of life, especially the more frivolous ones. For instance, everyone wears the same colourless clothes.

A more serious drawback is the lack of personal liberty. You cannot even travel about your own country without a special permit, and you have virtually no privacy. George Orwell's *Nineteen Eighty-Four*, with its telescreens in every room, and its slogan, BIG BROTHER IS WATCHING YOU, is merely a logical development from the situation in Utopia: 'Everyone has his eye on you, so you're practically forced to get on with your job, and make some proper use of your spare time' (p. 84).

To women, at least, the rigidly patriarchal character of Utopian society might prove a little tiresome. Once a month all wives have to kneel down before their husbands, 'confess all their sins of omission and commission, and ask to be for-given. This gets rid of any little grudges that may have clouded the domestic atmosphere . . .' (p. 126). But no provision is made for the domestic shortcomings of the male.

In sexual matters the penal code is barbarous. Pre-marital intercourse is punished by compulsory celibacy for life; adultery by slavery; and repeated adultery by death.

Noplacia, as Mr Windbag calls Utopia, is obviously no place to live, the average modern reader will decide; but to get a more stereoscopic view of it, one should make a momentary effort to see it through the eyes of its author, against a back-ground of Tudor England. More was himself a profoundly religious person, who subscribed unquestioningly to an authori-tarian code of morals, and was much attracted by the monastic

life. For four years in his youth he shared the living conditions
of the monks in the Charterhouse, and even after he had abandoned the idea of taking Holy Orders he secretly wore a hair-
shirt (which 'tamed his flesh till the blood was seen in his
clothes') until the day before he died. When he was sent to the
Tower in 1534, he almost welcomed the loss of comfort and
liberty, saying to his daughter:

I believe, Meg, that they that have put me here ween they have done
me a high displeasure. But I assure thee on my faith, my own good
daughter, if it had not been for my wife and you that be my children,
whom I account the chief part of my charge, I would not have failed
long ere this to have closed myself in as strait a room, and straiter
too . . . Me thinketh God maketh me a wanton [i.e. is spoiling me],
and setteth me on His lap and dandleth me.

(*Life* by William Roper, Oxford, 1935, p. 76.)

To a man of such habits and beliefs, the bareness and constric-
tion of life in Utopia must have seemed among its greatest
blessings.

Although he took great pains over his daughters' education,
he never seems to have regarded women as wholly rational
creatures. Erasmus says that when More was talking to a
woman, even if it was his own wife, he normally confined himself to making jokes. His view of sexual equality in the home
may perhaps be guessed from one of his Latin Epigrams, which
ends: 'If you let your wife stand on your toe tonight, she'll
stand on your face first thing tomorrow morning' (*Epigrammata*, 1520, p. 67, No. 140).

As for sexual intercourse, he evidently did not value it quite
as much as we do (he had not, of course, read any D. H.
Lawrence). On the contrary, he appeared to think it rather
ludicrous. Another early poem describes a rape. The lady
protests so much that finally the ravisher loses patience and
draws his sword.

'Now I warn you,' he said, 'if you don't shut up and lie down at
once, I'm off.'
Cowed by this fearful threat, the girl immediately lay down.
'All right, go ahead,' she said, 'but remember, you forced me
into it.'

(*Epigrammata*, 1520, p. 70, No. 149.)[2]

Erasmus helps us to understand More's attitude:

> When he was at the age for it, he had no objection to love-affairs with girls, but never overstepped the bounds of respectability; he enjoyed such things when they came his way, but did not go in search of them, and was more interested in mutual affection than in sexual inter-course.
>
> (*Erasmi Epistolae*, IV, Oxford, 1922, p. 17.)

From this R. W. Chambers deduces, rather oddly, that 'More was a man of strong passions' (*Thomas More*, London, 1935, p. 86). If so, they were kept well under control. He married his first wife out of 'a certain pity', although he felt more attracted to her younger sister; and he married again, Erasmus says, because he needed someone to look after his household, rather than from any idea of enjoying himself, 'for as he jokingly admits, she was neither young nor particularly pretty' (ibid., p. 19). In short, he was hardly the type to find much difficulty in observing the Utopian regulations about sex.

Finally we must remember what England was like when *Utopia* was written. It was a country where one individual could enjoy an income of £50,000 a year, while thousands of people starved, or were hanged for stealing food. For the abolition of such monstrous social injustice, a certain amount of austerity and regimentation might well seem a small price to pay. As for personal liberty, in Tudor England there was no freedom of speech; there was not even freedom of thought. More himself was executed, not for anything that he had said or done, but for private opinions which he had resolutely kept to himself. It was not enough to abstain from comment on Henry VIII's astonishing metamorphosis into Supreme Head of the Church: More's very silence was a political crime. Compared with the nightmarish quality of regal tyranny during the period, the pressure of public opinion in Utopia does not seem so very terrible; and if adulterers have a rather hard time there, at least they are not disembowelled alive, as More might easily have been, or, like three Carthusian monks convicted of the same crime, kept standing bolt upright in fetters and iron collars for seventeen days.

5

I shall make no further references here to the author's life. Its end is pretty well known, especially since Robert Bolt's *A Man for All Seasons*; and those who want a detailed biography should read (it practically reads itself) R. W. Chambers's *Thomas More* (London, 1935). I shall merely mention in the Notes a few biographical facts which are relevant to certain passages in the text.

6

More's *Utopia* gave its name to a literary genre, of which well over a hundred specimens have been published, the last in 1962; but the germ of Utopian fiction is probably to be found in ancient descriptions of paradise. In *The Epic of Gilgamesh*, Utnapishtim, the Sumerian equivalent of Noah, is discovered 'taking his ease on his back' in a place where

the croak of the raven was not heard, the bird of death did not utter the cry of death, the lion did not devour, the wolf did not tear the lamb, the dove did not mourn, there was no widow, no sickness, no old age, no lamentation.

(Penguin Translation, p. 39.)

In the *Odyssey* the description of the Elysian Fields stresses chiefly the superb weather-conditions; but Lucian, completing the picture later, represents Elysium as a luxurious holiday-camp, with honey and scent laid on, permanent background music provided by nightingales, and self-filling wine-glasses.

To this vein of pure wishful thinking Plato adds the element of serious political theory. In the *Republic* Socrates works out the idea of a perfect state, which embodies the principle of justice, and includes the communal ownership of goods and of women. The next stage in the development of the form is to give this airy nothing a local habitation and a name. In the *Timaeus* it is located on the island of Atlantis, which sank beneath the sea about nine thousand years before; and in the *Critias* the island is described in detail. It consists of several concentric rings of land, separated by circular canals which are so inter-connected that ships can sail right into the interior, and anchor there in underground harbours. Among other practical conveniences are two springs, one h. and one c., from which water is distributed all over the island through pipes attached, where necessary, to the bridges that cross the canals; and the outermost ring of land is very useful as a race-course.

A further ingredient in Utopian fiction is the fantastic traveller's tale, whether serious, as in Pliny's *Natural History*, or satirical, as in Lucian's *True History*. Many of the foreign tribes described by Pliny are remarkable only for their physique. Some have only one leg, which they use as a parasol in heat-waves; others have no mouths, and eat through their nostrils, with the help of a straw; others are born with white hair, which turns black as they grow old, and so on. But several are also remarkable for their customs. The Hyperborei practise euthanasia; the Garamantes are sexually promiscuous; the Esseni go to the opposite extreme:

Women they see none: carnal lust they know not: they handle no money: they lead their life by themselves, and keep company only with date trees.

(*Natural History*, v, 73 in Philemon Holland's translation, 1601.)

In Taprobane they have no laws or lawyers; in Babytace they hate gold so much that they bury it away out of sight; and there are people in India who have never been known to spit. Lucian, in a rather less earnest spirit, offers a sociological survey of the moon, where the all-male population wear clothes of flexible glass, feed on smoke, and think baldness very attractive.

Among such travellers' tales is one attributed to a certain Iambulus, which only survives in the history of Diodorus Siculus (II, 55–60). Iambulus is kidnapped by Ethiopians, who in accordance with an ancient tradition send him off in a boat with food for six months, to visit a 'happy island' in the South. After a mere four months of continuous storms, he duly arrives there. The island is circular, and inhabited by very tall, beautiful people with indiarubber bones. Among other natural advantages they have forked tongues, which enable them to carry on two conversations simultaneously. Normally they are never ill, so cripples and invalids get even less sympathy than they do in

Samuel Butler's *Erewhon*: they are compelled to practise euthanasia by lying down under a certain tree. The same applies to anyone who exceeds a statutory age-limit. They test their children's reactions in infancy, by sending them off for joy-rides on the backs of large birds: if the baby is airsick or terrified, they regard it as sub-standard, and expose it. As in Plato's *Republic*, women and children are public property.

More's technical contribution to the genre consisted in adding topical realism to the mixture of paradisiac, political, and travelogical elements already present in the story of Iambulus. In his unfinished *New Atlantis* (1626) Bacon added the element of dramatic tension. He imaginatively describes the first approach to the island of Bensalem, injecting it with a powerful dose of anxiety and bewilderment; for although the narrator and his companions are on the point of starvation, they are not immediately allowed to land, and have to go through some rather discouraging immigration-formalities. Bacon also replaces Raphael's logically organized account of Utopia recollected in tranquillity by a narrative tracing his visitors' gradual acquisition of knowledge about Bensalem, from the moment when they sight what looks like land on the horizon, to the moment when the Principal of the local Institute for Scientific Research concludes his report of work in progress, and presents his audience with two thousand ducats (perhaps as a reward for listening so attentively). The only real precedent for this piece of Utopian technique is to be found in the *Christianopolis* (1619) of J. V. Andreae, which starts rather too allegorically with a voyage in the good ship Fantasy across the Academic Ocean, but suddenly comes to life when Andreae is wrecked on a triangular island, and shortly afterwards discovered by a coastguard trying to dry his shirt in the sun.

Meanwhile Joseph Hall had invented the so-called Dystopia. In his *Mundus Alter et Idem* (Another World and yet the Same, 1600) he described a voyage, also on board the Fantasy, to various countries in the Southern Hemisphere which satirized their opposite numbers in the Northern. For instance, in Pamphagonia and Yvronia, which have the same latitudes and longitudes as England and Germany respectively, the principal industries are eating and drinking. Pamphagonia contains

a town called Marzipan, whose inhabitants all suffer from
dental caries and halitosis, and another where full citizenship
is granted only to those with stomach-measurements above a
statutory minimum. In Yvronia every man has a special rope,
with rings attached at convenient intervals, leading from the
market-place to his own house, so that he can find his way
home after parties; occasionally these ropes get tied on to the
wrong houses, with consequent matrimonial complications.
Hall's satire is mostly pretty light-hearted, but his book created
a sub-species which includes works as savage as *Gulliver's
Travels* (1726), as profound as *Erewhon* (1872), and as horrifying
as Aldous Huxley's *Brave New World* (1932) and *Ape and
Essence* (1949), or George Orwell's barely endurable *Nineteen
Eighty-Four* (1949).

Utopias have been written to illustrate many different theories
of perfection. In *Christianopolis* the secret of happiness is true
religion; in William Morris's *News from Nowhere* (1890) it is
socialism. In Samuel Gott's *New Jerusalem* (1648) it is education: teachers at the university get 'maximum salaries', and the
students take down lecture-notes in shorthand. In Tommaso
Campanella's *City of the Sun* (1623) the good life is largely a
matter of eugenics: though male adolescents are allowed to
copulate freely with sterile or pregnant women, all reproduc-
tive mating is government-controlled. The use of cosmetics is
a capital crime, possibly because it might have the effect of
attracting males to eugenically unsuitable females.

New Atlantis, with its inventions foreshadowing such things
as aircraft, submarines, radiograms, and telephones, embodies
a faith in the blessings of science which is echoed in Edward
Bellamy's *Looking Backward* (1887), where the possibility of
getting orchestral music on the telephone is considered almost
enough in itself to make Boston, Mass., a paradise:

'It appears to me, Miss Leete,' I said, 'that if we could have devised an arrangement for providing everybody with music in their
homes, perfect in quality, unlimited in quantity, suited to every
mood and beginning and ceasing at will, we should have considered
the limit of human felicity already attained, and ceased to strive for
further improvements.'   (pp. 157–8)

Science also contributes largely to human felicity in Aldous

Huxley's *Island* (1962), for instance, by saving fathers the trouble of staying alive:

> 'Well, that's the man we chose for Rama's father.'
> 'But I understood he was dead.'
> Shanta nodded. 'But his soul goes marching along.'
> 'What do you mean?'
> 'DF and AI.'
> 'DF and AI?'
> 'Deep Freeze and Artificial Insemination.' (p. 187)

The old-fashioned method of getting to Utopia is to be wrecked on an island, preferably in the South Seas, and Huxley's last essay in the genre is to this extent traditional. So is William Golding's *Lord of the Flies* (1954), which may, I think, be considered a rather individual form of Dystopia. The substitution of a plane-crash for a shipwreck has a precedent in James Hilton's *Lost Horizon* (1933), where the plane is piloted by a sinister stranger with a revolver. He kidnaps a party of airline passengers, and lands them somewhat heavily among the snows of Tibet, but within walking-distance of Shangri-La, a centenarians' paradise which reminds the hero 'very slightly of Oxford' (p. 212).

For some time, however, Utopia-writers have been faced by the increasingly awkward problem, where on earth to put their undiscovered countries? Lord Lytton solved it in *The Coming Race* (1871) by not putting his Utopia on earth at all, but under it. While investigating a charred and jagged chasm in a new shaft of a mine, an engineer is surprised to see a row of street-lamps leading away into the distance. Soon afterwards he is eaten by a peculiarly ferocious subterranean monster; but an American friend of his survives, and walks down the street into the country of the Vril-Ya. Here society is dominated by females seven feet tall, with 'grand but unalluring countenances' (p. 224) and, possibly for this reason, extra-marital relations are unheard of.

Another solution is to distance your Utopia, not in space, but in time. Since Plato, nobody has been so retrogressive as to place it in the past, but it is often placed in the future. One gets there either by dreaming (*News from Nowhere*), or by over-sleeping (*Looking Backward*, and H. G. Wells's *When the Sleeper*

Wakes, 1899), or by operating a special apparatus (H. G. Wells's *The Time Machine*, 1895), or by an involuntary exchange of bodies with some unscrupulous member of posterity (John Wyndham's *Pillar to Post*, 1956); or else one is not a visitor at all but a permanent resident, like the bearded heroine of Evelyn Waugh's *Love among the Ruins* (1953).

In the last resort, Utopias and Dystopias can always be located on another planet. *The First Men in the Moon* (1901) by H. G. Wells gives a highly satirical account of Selenite society, in which the intellectuals have enormous swollen heads and tiny stunted bodies, and the workers are drugged into a state of coma, whenever they are not required for work. A rather more flattering picture of the Lunars is presented by Francis Godwin's *The Man in the Moon* (1638). Under the pseudonym of Domingo Gonsales, this enterprising Bishop travelled to the Moon on an 'Engine' powered by twenty-five wild swans, each fitted with a special pulley and counterweight to ensure that it did not carry more than its fair share of episcopal avoirdupois. There he found some people of a very curious colour, who had no lawyers, no crime, and no infidelity – for the women were so exquisitely beautiful that once you had known one of them you never wanted to look at any other, and criminal types were recognized in early childhood and instantly deported to the Earth:

Their ordinary vent for them is a certain high hill in the North of America, whose people I can easily believe to be wholly descended of them, partly in regard of their colour, partly also in regard of the continuous use of Tobacco, which the Lunars use exceeding much... (p. 105)

In Mary McCarthy's *A Source of Embarrassment* (1950) three trespassers ruin the morale of a Utopian colony, somewhere in the U.S.A., by shamelessly picking the colony's strawberries. They must have been rejects from the Moon.

7

The translation is based on the text of the first edition (1516), though I have incorporated (on page 86) a half-sentence which

was not printed until two years later. Of the letters, verses, etc.,
published with the original text I have included only those
which are part of the practical joke. Among them are the lines
by Mr Windbag, which are obviously meant to be silly (though
some critics have discovered profound meaning in them), and
by their prominent position on the fourth page to establish the
April Fool atmosphere right from the start. I flatter myself that
my version is quite as silly as the original.

The material omitted consists of a letter and some verses by
John Van der Broeck, Professor of Rhetoric at Louvain (where
the book was printed), and of a letter by Jerome Busleiden, the
addressee of the letter from Peter Gilles. Van der Broeck's contribution is of no particular interest, and was excluded from the
edition of 1518; Busleiden's is interesting only because he seems
to take Utopia literally, as a model of political organization, not
symbolically, as a mere moral fable.

8

Several of my friends, on hearing that I was translating *Utopia*,
have looked faintly puzzled and asked: 'Into what?' Educated
people are often unaware that the book was written in Latin,
and many imagine that they have read the original, when what
they have actually read is Ralph Robinson's translation (1551).
This is rather a pity, because the great merits of Robinson's version, its liveliness and readability, have now largely evaporated
for those who are unfamiliar with sixteenth-century English,
and his archaic idiom is liable to obscure More's perfectly plain
meaning.

Some such obscurity is inevitable when a sixteenth-century
author writes in English; but when he writes in Latin, it is
quite unnecessary. For hundreds of years Latin served as a
universal language through which one could speak directly,
not only to people of other nationalities, but to people of other
periods as well. *Utopia* is expressed in a timeless medium, which
cuts it loose from its own particular age, and saves it from ever
seeming linguistically old-fashioned or difficult.

I have therefore thought it my business to convey the effect
of this temporal Esperanto, by using the sort of idiom which

would interfere as little as possible with the entry of More's ideas into a modern mind. I have tried especially to render his social and economic arguments, which are so much a part of our intellectual atmosphere, into language that is equally close to us.

Then there were the demands of the fictional context. Most of the work is supposed to be spoken aloud: Book II is a 'talk' improvised on the spur of the moment, and Book I is mainly concerned with recording an informal conversation. In order to make all this spoken material speakable, I have freely used colloquial phrases and abbreviations, broken up long, complex sentences into short, simple ones, and replaced the nine chapter headings in Book II (e.g. 'About trades', 'About warfare', 'About the travelling of the Utopians') by the more relaxed type of subject-changing formula dear to the lecturer or broadcaster who pretends to be improvising.

The only other liberty that I am conscious of having taken is very occasionally eliminating tautology, when I thought that the modern reader would immediately grasp the meaning without it; but for this perhaps I can quote the authority of More himself: 'I have no wish to labour the obvious' (p. 37).

P.D.L.T.

NOTES

Proper names invented by More have normally been Anglicized in the translation. The originals are to be found in the Glossary, together with etymological explanations. Any name which does not appear in the Glossary (e.g. Raphael, Barzanes, Utopia) may be assumed to have retained its original form.

THE UTOPIAN ALPHABET

A Specimen of Utopian Poetry

ⒷⒿⓁⒻⓁⒽ ⒸⓄ ⒽⓁⓄⓂⓄⒽ ⓁⒼⒽ ⒺⓄ ⓂⒸⓄⒹⓄ ⓁⓁⒺⒿⓄ ⓂⒸⓄⒹⓄⓄⒿ
ⒽⓄⒹⒹⓁⒺ ⒸⒼ ⒹⓄⒿⒺⓁⒹ⏀ ⒽⓄⓂⓂⓄⒿ ⒷⓁⒹⓄ ⒿⒺⒶⒿⓁⒽⓁⓁⒼⓄⓁⒿ
ⓄⒿⓄⓄⒹ ⒿⒺⒶⒿⓁⒽⓁⓁⒼⓁⒿ ⒺⓄⒽⓄⓄⒼⒹⒽⓄⓂⒸⓄ ⒽⓁⓄⓄⒹ⏀ⒺⓁⒹ⏀
ⒷⓁⒺⒽⓄⒺⓄ ⒽⓄⒹⒹⓂⒸ⏀Ⓙ ⒸⒼⒹⓄⒿ ⒺⓄ ⒺⓄⒽⓁⒺⒽⓁⒺⓄ ⓄⒹⓄⒹⒹⓄ ⓁⓄⒿⒺⓁⒿ⏀

The Same Transliterated

Utopos ha Boccas peu la chama polta chamaan.
Bargol he maglomi baccan soma gymnosophaon
Agrama gymnosophon labarembacha bodamilomin.
Volvala barchin heman, la lavolvola dramme pagloni.[3]

A Word-for-Word Translation

Utopos me General[4] from not island made island.
Alone I of-lands all without philosophy
State philosophical[5] I-have-formed for-mortals.
Willingly I-impart my-things, not not-willingly I-accept better-ones.

*Lines on the Island of Utopia by
the Poet Laureate, Mr Windbag*[6]
Nonsenso's sister's son

NOPLACIA was once my name,
That is, a place where no one goes.
Plato's *Republic* now I claim
To match, or beat at its own game;
For that was just a myth in prose,
But what he wrote of, I became,
Of men, wealth, laws a solid frame,
A place where every wise man goes:
GOPLACIA[7] is now my name.

My dear Peter Gilles, [8]

I feel almost ashamed to send you this little book about the Utopian Republic, for I've kept you waiting for nearly a year, and you doubtless expected to get it within six weeks. You knew that in this work I didn't have the problem of finding my own subject-matter and puzzling out a suitable form – all I had to do was repeat what Raphael told us. There was no need to bother very much about the wording, since his style wasn't particularly polished – the whole thing was improvised on the spur of the moment, and, as you know, his Latin isn't quite as good as his Greek. So the closer I could get to his simple, off-hand way of expressing himself, the closer I'd be to the truth, which in this case is all I'm worrying about, and all I ought to worry about.

Yes, Peter, I know. So much of it was ready made, that there was practically nothing left for me to do. Mind you, in any other circumstances the creation and organization of a thing like this would have demanded a good deal of time and thought – even from a reasonably intelligent and cultivated person. And if the style had had to be graceful as well as accurate, no amount of time and thought would have enabled me to do it. As it was, I was relieved of all such headaches. My job was simply to write down what I'd heard, which was really perfectly easy – but my other commitments have left me less than no time to get this perfectly easy job done. I've been kept hard at work in the law courts, [9] either at the Bar or on the Bench, either in civil or in criminal cases. Then there's always someone that has to be visited, either on business, or as a matter of courtesy. I'm out practically all day, dealing with other people – the rest of the day I spend with my family – so there's no time left for me, that is, for my writing.

You see, when I come home, I've got to talk to my wife, have a chat with my children, and discuss things with my servants. I count this as one of my commitments, because it's absolutely necessary, if I'm not to be a stranger in my own home. Besides, one should always try to be nice to the people one lives with, whether one has chosen their company deliberately, or merely been thrown into it by chance or family-relationship – that is, as nice as one can without spoiling them, or turning servants into masters.

Thus the days, the months, the years slip by. You may ask, when *do* I write then? Well, so far I haven't mentioned sleep, or meals – which many people allow to consume as much time as sleep itself – and in fact the only time I ever get to myself is what I steal from sleep and meals. There isn't very much of it, so my progress has been slow – but there has at least been some, so I've finally finished *Utopia*, and I'm sending it to you, my dear Peter, in the hope that you will read it, and tell me if I've left anything out. I feel fairly confident on that score – for I only wish my scholarship and intelligence were up to the standard of my memory – but not quite confident enough to assume that nothing could have slipped my mind.

As you know, my young assistant, John Clement,[10] was with us at the time. I never let him miss any conversation that might have some educational value, for he has already begun to show such promise in Latin and Greek that I expect great things of him one day. Well, he has made me feel very doubtful about one point. As far as I can recall, Raphael told us that the bridge across the river Nowater at Aircastle was five hundred yards long, but John wants me to reduce this number by two hundred, for he says the river wasn't more than three hundred yards wide at that point. Will you please search your memory for the correct figure? If you agree with him, I'll take your word for it, and assume that I've made a mistake. But if you've completely forgotten, I'll let my figure stand, for that's how I seem to remember it. You see, I'm extremely anxious to get my facts right, and, when in doubt, any lies that I tell will be quite unintentional, for I'd much rather be thought honest than clever.

However, the simplest solution would be for you to ask Raphael himself, either by word of mouth or by letter – in fact you must do that anyway, because of another little problem which has cropped up. I don't know whose fault it was, mine, yours, or Raphael's, but we never thought of asking, and he never thought of telling us whereabouts in the New World Utopia is. I'd gladly give what little money I possess to repair the omission. For one thing, it makes me feel rather a fool, after all I've written about the island, not to know what sea it's in. For another, there are one or two people in England who want to go there. In particular, there's a very pious theologian,[11] who's desperately keen to visit Utopia, not in a spirit of idle curiosity, but so that he can foster the growth of Christianity, now that it's been successfully introduced into that country. As he wishes to do it officially, he has decided to get himself sent out there by the Pope, and actually created Bishop of Utopia. He's not deterred by any scruples about begging for preferment.[12] He thinks that sort of thing is perfectly all right if it's done, not for the sake of profit or prestige, but purely out of zeal.

So, Peter, will you please arrange to see Raphael, if you conveniently can, or else write to him, and make sure that my work contains the whole truth and nothing but the truth? Perhaps it would be best for you to show him the book itself, for he's the person best qualified to correct any mistakes, and he can't very well do so, unless he reads the thing right through. Besides, in that way you'll be able to find out how he reacts to the idea of my writing up the results of his researches. For if he's planning to write them up himself, he'd probably rather I didn't – and I certainly shouldn't want to give Utopia premature publicity, so that his story lost the charm of novelty.

To tell you the truth, though, I still haven't made up my mind whether I shall publish it at all. Tastes differ so widely, and some people are so humourless, so uncharitable, and so absurdly wrong-headed, that one would probably do far better to relax and enjoy life than worry oneself to death trying to instruct or entertain a public which will only despise one's efforts, or at least feel no gratitude for them. Most readers know nothing about literature – many regard it with contempt. Lowbrows find everything heavy going that isn't completely lowbrow. Highbrows reject everything as vulgar that isn't a mass of archaisms. Some only like the classics, others only their own works. Some are so grimly serious that they disapprove of all humour, others so half-witted that they can't stand wit. Some are so literal-minded that the slightest hint of irony affects them as water affects a sufferer from hydrophobia. Others come to different conclusions every time they stand up or sit down. Then there's the alcoholic school of critics, who sit in public houses, pronouncing *ex cathedra* verdicts of condemnation, just as they think fit. They seize upon your publications, as a wrestler seizes upon his opponent's hair, and use them to drag you down, while they themselves remain quite invulnerable, because their barren pates are completely bald – so there's nothing for you to get hold of.

Besides, some readers are so ungrateful that, even if they enjoy a book immensely, they don't feel any affection for the author. They're like rude guests who after a splendid dinner-party go home stuffed with food, without saying a word of thanks to their host. So much for the wisdom of preparing a feast of reason at one's own expense for a public with such fastidious and unpredictable tastes, and with such a profound sense of gratitude!

But do, as I say, get in touch with Raphael. I can think about the other question later – though really it's too late to start being sensible now, when I've gone to all the trouble of writing the book. So if he has no objection, whether I publish it or not will depend on what my friends, and especially what you advise.

Best wishes, my dearest Peter Gilles, to you and your charming wife. And please go on liking me as much as ever – because I like you even more than ever.

Yours sincerely,
THOMAS MORE

Antwerp
1 November 1516

My dear Busleiden,[13]

The other day a great friend of yours, Thomas More – who is, I'm sure you'll agree, one of the glories of our age – sent me the enclosed account of Utopia. At present very few people know about this island, but everyone should want to, for it's like Plato's *Republic*, only better – especially as it's described by such a talented author. He sets it all so vividly before one's eyes that by reading his words I seem to get an even clearer picture of it than I did while Raphael Nonsenso's voice was actually sounding in my ears – for I was with More when the conversation took place. And yet Raphael spoke extraordinarily well. He obviously wasn't retailing somebody else's story, but describing his own experiences in a place where he'd lived for quite a long time. Personally, I think he must have seen even more of the world than Ulysses, and I doubt if there has been anyone like him for at least eight hundred years. He made us feel that Vespucci had seen absolutely nothing!

The man also appeared to have a special talent for exposition – though I suppose we can always describe what we've seen more effectively than what we've heard. But when I consider More's quasi-pictorial treatment of the same theme, I sometimes get the impression that I'm actually living in Utopia. In fact, I honestly believe there's more to be seen in his account of the island than Raphael himself can have seen during all those five years that he spent there. One comes across so many wonderful things on every page, that I hardly know what to admire first or most – the remarkable accuracy of his memory, which could reproduce an immensely long speech practically word for word – his cleverness in immediately grasping the actual and potential causes, hitherto largely unknown, of every social evil – or the force and fluency of his style, his ability to deal with such a variety of topics in such correct and muscular Latin – especially as he's distracted by so many official and domestic responsibilities. But all this will seem less surprising to a fine scholar like you. Besides, you already know him intimately, and are quite familiar with the prodigious, if not positively superhuman power of his intellect.

I can't think of anything to add to what he has written – except that I've attached four lines of verse in the Utopian language, which Nonsenso happened to show me after More had gone, together with the Utopian alphabet. I've also added a few marginal notes.[14] By the way, More's a bit worried because he doesn't know the exact position of the island. As a matter of fact Raphael did mention it, but only very briefly and incidentally, as though he meant to return to the question later – and, for some unknown reason, we were both fated to miss it. You see, just as Raphael was touching on the subject, a servant came up to More and whispered something in his ear. And although this made me listen with even greater attention, at the critical moment one of his colleagues started coughing rather loudly – I suppose he'd caught cold on the boat – so that the rest of Raphael's sentence was completely inaudible. However, I shan't rest until I've cleared up that point too, and can tell you exactly where the island is, latitude and all. That is, if our friend Raphael is still safe and sound, for I've heard several different stories about him. Some people say that he has died somewhere on his travels. Others that he has gone back to his own country. Others again that he has returned to Utopia, partly because he felt nostalgic about it, and partly because he couldn't stand the way Europeans behaved.

You may wonder why no reference to Utopia appears in any geographical work, but this problem has been very neatly solved by Raphael himself. He says it's quite possible that the ancients knew of the island under another name, or else that they never heard of it at all – for nowadays countries are always being discovered which were never mentioned in the old geography books. However, I need no arguments to prove my point, when I can appeal to the authority of a man like More.

I understand and respect the modesty that makes him hesitate to publish. Personally, though, I think it's the sort of work that should on no account be suppressed for long, but should be put into circulation as quickly as possible, preferably with a letter from you to recommend it to the world – because you have a special insight into More's genius, and who could be better qualified to introduce sound ideas to the public than one who has spent many years in the public service and earned the highest praise for his wisdom and integrity?

With all good wishes to a great patron of scholarship, who is also among the glories of this age,

Yours sincerely,
PETER GILLES

BOOK ONE

THERE was recently a rather serious difference of opinion[1] between that great expert in the art of government, His Invincible Majesty, King Henry the Eighth of England, and His Serene Highness, Prince Charles of Castile. His Majesty sent me to Flanders to discuss and settle the matter, along with my friend Cuthbert Tunstall,[2] an excellent person who has since been appointed Master of the Rolls, much to everyone's satisfaction. Of his learning and moral character I shall say nothing – not because I am afraid of seeming prejudiced in his favour, but because they are too remarkable for me to describe adequately, and too well known to need describing at all. I have no wish to labour the obvious.[3]

We were met at Bruges, as previously arranged, by the envoys from Castile, who were all men of great distinction. Their nominal leader was the Mayor of Bruges, and a splendid fellow he was; but most of the thinking and talking was done by the Provost of Cassel, George de Theimsecke. This man was a born speaker, as well as a highly trained one. He was also a legal expert, and both by temperament and by long experience a first-rate negotiator. After one or two meetings there were still some points on which we had failed to agree, so they said goodbye to us for a few days and set off for Brussels, to consult their royal oracle. In the meantime I went to Antwerp on business of my own.

While I was there, I had several frequent visitors, but the one I liked best was a young native of Antwerp called Peter Gilles. He is much respected by his own people, and holds an important post in that town; but he fully deserves promotion to the highest post of all, for I do not know which impressed me more, his intellectual or his moral qualities. Certainly he is a very fine person, as well as a very fine scholar. He is scrupulously fair to everyone, but towards his friends he shows so much genuine kindness, loyalty, and affection, that he must be almost unique in his all-round capacity for friendship. He is unusually modest, utterly sincere, and has a shrewd simplicity all his own. He is also a delightful talker, who can be witty without hurting anyone's feelings. I was longing to get back to England and see my wife and children, as I had been away for over four months; but my homesickness was to a large extent relieved by the pleasure of his company and the charm of his conversation.

One day I had been to a service at the Cathedral of Notre Dame, a magnificent building which is always packed with people. I was just starting back to my hotel when I happened to see Peter Gilles talking to an elderly foreigner with a sunburnt face, a long beard, and a cloak slung carelessly over one shoulder.⁴ From his complexion and costume I judged him to be a sailor. At this point Peter caught sight of me. He immediately came up and said good morning, then before I had time to reply, drew me a little further away.

'Do you see that man over there?' he asked, indicating the one he had been talking to. 'I was just bringing him along to visit you.'

'If he's a friend of yours,' I said, 'I'll be very glad to see him.'

'When you hear the sort of person he is,' said Peter, 'you'll be glad to see him anyway – for there's not a man alive today who can tell you so many stories about strange countries and their inhabitants as he can. I know what a passion you have for that kind of thing.'

'Then I didn't guess too far wrong,' I remarked. 'The moment I saw him, I thought he must be a sailor.'

'In that case you made a big mistake,' he replied. 'I mean, he's not a sailor of the Palinurus⁵ type. He's really more like Ulysses, or even Plato. You see, our friend Raphael – for that's his name, Raphael Nonsenso⁶ – is quite a scholar. He knows a fair amount of Latin and a tremendous lot of Greek. He's concentrated on Greek, because he's mainly interested in philosophy, and he found that there's nothing important on that subject written in Latin, apart from some bits of Seneca and Cicero. He wanted to see the world, so he left his brothers to manage his property in Portugal – that's where he comes from – and joined up with Amerigo Vespucci.⁷ You know those *Four Voyages*⁸ of his that everyone's reading about? Well, Raphael was his constant companion during the last three, except that he didn't come back

with him from the final voyage. Instead, he practically forced
Amerigo to let him be one of the twenty-four men who were
left behind in that fort.⁹ So he stayed out there, to indulge his
taste for travel, which was all he really cared about. He didn't
mind where he eventually died, for he had two favourite quotations, "The unburied dead are covered by the sky"¹⁰ and "You
can get to heaven from anywhere"¹¹ – an attitude which, but
for the grace of God, might have led to serious trouble. Anyway, when Vespucci had gone, Raphael did a lot of exploring
with five other members of the garrison. Finally, by an amazing
stroke of luck, they turned up in Ceylon. From there he made
his way to Calicut, where he was fortunate enough to find some
Portuguese ships, and so, quite unexpectedly, got a passage
home.'

'Well, thank you very much,' I said. 'I'll certainly enjoy talking to a man like that. It's most kind of you to give me a chance
of doing so.'

I then walked up to Raphael and shook hands with him. After
making a few stock remarks, as people generally do when first
introduced, we adjourned to the garden of my hotel, where we
sat down on a bench covered with a layer of turf, and began to
talk more freely.

First of all Raphael told us what happened to him and the
other men in the fort, from the point where Vespucci left them.
By polite and friendly behaviour they gradually started ingrati-
ating themselves with the local inhabitants. Soon relations were
not merely peaceful but positively affectionate. They got on
particularly well with a certain king, whose name and nation-
ality have slipped my memory. He most generously provided
Raphael and his five fellow-explorers with food and money
for their journeys, which involved the use of boats as well as
carriages. He also supplied a most reliable guide, who was told
to put them in touch with various other kings, to whom they
were given letters of introduction. Thus after travelling for
many days they came to some large towns and densely popu-
lated areas, with quite a high standard of political organization.

Apparently, at the equator, and throughout most of the tor-
rid zone, you find vast deserts parched by perpetual heat. Everything looks grim and desolate. There are no signs of cultivation,

and no animal life, except for snakes and wild beasts, or equally wild and dangerous human beings. But, if you go on a bit further, things gradually improve. The climate becomes less extreme, the earth grows green and pleasant, human beings and animals are not so fierce. Finally, you come to people living in towns and cities, who are constantly engaged in trade, both by land and by sea, not only with one another or with their immediate neighbours, but even with quite distant countries.

'This gave me the chance,' said Raphael, 'of travelling about all over the place, for whenever I found a ship just setting sail I asked if my friends and I might go on board, and they were always glad to let us. The first ships we saw were flat-bottomed, with sails made of papyrus leaves stitched together, or else of wicker-work, or in some cases of leather. But the ones we came across later had sharp keels and canvas sails, and were generally just like ours. The sailors out there have a good knowledge of winds and tides, but I made myself extraordinarily popular with them by explaining the use of the magnetic compass. They'd never heard of it before, and for that reason had always been rather frightened of the sea, and seldom risked going on it except during the summer. But now they put such faith in their compasses that they think nothing of winter voyages – although this new sense of security is purely subjective. In fact their over-confidence threatens to convert an apparently useful invention into a source of disaster.'

It would take too long to repeat everything he told us about each place. Besides, that is not the purpose of this book. I may conceivably do so in another one, emphasizing the most instructive parts of his story, such as the sensible arrangements that he noticed in various civilized communities. These were the points on which we questioned him most closely, and he enlarged most willingly. We did not ask him if he had seen any monsters, for monsters have ceased to be news. There is never any shortage of horrible creatures who prey on human beings, snatch away their food, or devour whole populations;[12] but examples of wise social planning are not so easy to find.

Of course, he saw much to condemn in the New World, but he also discovered several regulations which suggested possible methods of reforming European society. These, I say, will have to be dealt with later. My present plan is merely to repeat what he said about the laws and customs of Utopia.

I must start by recording the conversation which led up to the first mention of that republic. After shrewdly pointing out the mistakes that have been made on both sides of the globe – and there are certainly plenty of them – Raphael went on to discuss the more sensible features of Old and New World legislation. He seemed to have the facts about every single country at his finger-tips – as though he had spent a lifetime wherever he had stopped for a night. Peter Gilles was particularly impressed.

PETER:[13] My dear Raphael, I can't think why you don't enter the service of some king[14] or other. I'm sure any king would jump at the chance of employing you. With your knowledge and experience, you'd be just the man to supply not only entertainment, but also instructive precedents and useful advice. At the same time you could be looking after your own interests, and being a great help to all your friends and relations.

RAPHAEL: I'm not really worried about them. I feel I've done my duty by them already. Most people hang on to their property until they're too old and ill to do so any longer – and even then they relinquish it with a very ill grace. But I shared out mine among my friends and relations when I was still young and healthy. I think they should be satisfied with that. They can hardly expect me to go a stage further, and become a king's slave for their benefit.

PETER: God forbid! Service, not servitude, was what I suggested.

RAPHAEL: A few letters don't make all that difference.

PETER: Well, call it what you like, I still think it's your best method of helping other people, both individually and collectively, and also of making life pleasanter for yourself.

RAPHAEL: How can I do that by acting against all my instincts? At present I live exactly as I please, which is more, I suspect, than the vast majority of court officials can say. Besides, kings have quite enough people competing for their friendship already. It won't be any serious hardship for them to do without me, and a handful of others like me.

MORE: My dear Raphael, you're obviously not interested in money or power, and I couldn't respect you more if you were the greatest king on earth. But surely it would be quite in keeping with this admirably philosophical attitude if you could bring yourself, even at the cost of some personal inconvenience, to apply your talents and energies to public affairs? Now the most effective way of doing so would be to gain the confidence of some great king or other, and give him, as I know you would, really good advice. For every king is a sort of fountain, from which a constant shower of benefits or injuries rains down upon the whole population. And you've got so much theoretical knowledge, and so much practical experience, that either of them alone would be enough to make you an ideal member of any privy council.

RAPHAEL: You're quite mistaken, my dear More, first about me and then about the job itself. I'm not so highly qualified as you seem to think, and, even if I were, I still shouldn't do the slightest good to the community by giving myself a lot of extra work. To start with, most kings are more interested in the science of war – which I don't know anything about, and don't want to – than in useful peacetime techniques. They're far more anxious, by hook or by crook, to acquire new kingdoms than to govern their existing ones properly. Besides, privy councillors are either too wise to need, or too conceited to take advice from anyone else – though of course they're always prepared to suck up to the king's special favourites by agreeing with the silliest things they say. After all, it's a natural instinct to be charmed by one's own productions. That's why raven chicks are such a delight to their parents, and mother apes find their babies exquisitely beautiful.

So there you have a group of people who are deeply prejudiced against everyone else's ideas, or at any rate prefer their own. Suppose, in such company, you suggest a policy that you've seen adopted elsewhere, or for which you can quote a historical precedent, what will happen? They'll behave as though their professional reputations were at stake, and they'd look fools for the rest of their lives if they couldn't raise some objection to your proposal. Failing all else, their last resort will be: 'This was good enough for our ancestors, and who are we to question their wisdom?' Then they'll settle back in their chairs, with an air of having said the last word on the subject –

as if it would be a major disaster for anyone to be caught being wiser than his ancestors! And yet we're quite prepared to reverse their most sensible decisions. It's only the less intelligent ones that we cling on to like grim death. I've come across this curious mixture of conceit, stupidity, and stubbornness in several different places. On one occasion I even met it in England.

MORE: Really? Have you been to my country too, then?

RAPHAEL: Certainly I have. I was there for several months, soon after that disastrous civil war which began with a revolution[15] in the west country, and ended with a ghastly massacre of the rebels. During my stay, I received a lot of kindness from the Most Reverend John Morton,[16] the Archbishop of Canterbury. He was also a Cardinal, and at that time Lord Chancellor of England. I must tell you about him, Peter – for I can't tell More anything he doesn't know already. He was a person that one respected just as much for his wisdom and moral character as for his great eminence. He was of average height, without a trace of a stoop, although he was fairly old. He had the sort of face that inspires reverence rather than fear. He was quite easy to get on with, though always serious and dignified. Admittedly he was rather inclined to be rude to people who asked him for jobs, but he meant no harm by it. He only did it to test their intelligence and presence of mind, for he found these qualities very congenial, so long as they were used with discretion, and considered them most valuable in public life. He was a polished and effective speaker, with a thorough knowledge of the law. He also had a quite remarkable intellect, and a phenomenal memory – two natural gifts which he'd further developed by training and practice.

Apparently the King had great confidence in his judgement, and at the time of my visit the whole country seemed to depend on him. This was hardly surprising, since he'd been rushed straight from the university to Court, when he was not much more than a boy, and had spent the rest of his life in the public service, learning wisdom the hard way, by having to cope with a long series of crises. And what one learns like that isn't easily forgotten.

I once happened to be dining with the Cardinal when a certain English lawyer was there. I forgot how the subject came up, but he was speaking with great enthusiasm about the stern measures that were then being taken against thieves.

'We're hanging them all over the place,' he said, 'I've seen as many as twenty on a single gallows. And that's what I find so odd. Considering how few of them get away with it, why are we still plagued with so many robbers?'

'What's odd about it?' I asked – for I never hesitated to speak freely in front of the Cardinal. 'This method of dealing with thieves is both unjust and socially undesirable. As a punishment it's too severe, and as a deterrent it's quite ineffective. Petty larceny isn't bad enough to deserve the death penalty, and no penalty on earth will stop people from stealing, if it's their only way of getting food. In this respect you English, like most other nations, remind me of incompetent schoolmasters, who prefer caning their pupils to teaching them. Instead of inflicting these horrible punishments, it would be far more to the point to provide everyone with some means of livelihood, so that nobody's under the frightful necessity of becoming first a thief and then a corpse.'

'There's adequate provision for that already,' replied the lawyer. 'There are plenty of trades open to them. There's always work on the land. They could easily earn an honest living if they wanted to, but they deliberately choose to be criminals.'

'You can't get out of it like that,' I said. 'Let's ignore, for the sake of argument, the case of the disabled soldier, who has lost a limb in the service of King and Country, either at home or abroad – perhaps in that battle with the Cornish rebels, or perhaps during the fighting in France,[17] not so long ago. When he comes home, he finds he's physically incapable of practising his former trade, and too old to learn a new one. But as I say, let's forget about him, since war is only an intermittent phenomenon. Let's stick to the type of thing that happens every day.

'Well, first of all there are lots of noblemen who live like drones on the labour of other people, in other words, of their tenants, and keep bleeding them white by constantly raising their rents. For that's their only idea of practical economy – otherwise they'd soon be ruined by their extravagance. But not content with remaining idle themselves, they take round with them vast numbers of equally idle retainers, who have never been taught any method of earning their living. The moment their master dies, or they themselves fall ill, they're promptly given the sack – for these noblemen are far more sympathetic towards idleness than illness, and their heirs often can't afford to keep up such large establishments. Now a sacked retainer is apt to get violently hungry, if he doesn't resort to violence. For what's the alternative? He can, of course, wander around until his clothes and his body are both worn out, and he's nothing but a mass of rags and sores. But in that state no gentleman will condescend to employ him, and no farmer can risk doing so – for who could be less likely to serve a poor man faithfully, sweating away with mattock and hoe for a beggarly wage and a barely adequate diet, than a man who has been brought up in the lap of luxury, and is used to swaggering about in military uniform, looking down his nose at everyone else in the neighbourhood?'

'But that's exactly the kind of person we need to encourage,' retorted the lawyer. 'In wartime he forms the backbone of the army, simply because he has more spirit and self-respect than an ordinary tradesman or farm-hand.'

'You might as well say,' I answered, 'that for purposes of war you have to encourage theft. Well, you'll certainly never run short of thieves, so long as you have people like that about. And, of course, you're perfectly right – thieves do make quite efficient soldiers, and soldiers make quite enterprising thieves. The two professions have a good deal in common. However, the trouble is not confined to England, although you've got it pretty badly. It's practically a world-wide epidemic. France, for instance, is suffering from an even more virulent form of it. There the whole country is overrun even in peacetime – if you can call it that – by mercenaries who have been brought in for much the same reasons as you gave for supporting idle retainers. You see, the experts decided, in the interests of public safety, that they must have a powerful standing army, consisting mostly of veterans – for they put so little faith in raw recruits that they deliberately start wars to give their soldiers practice, and make them cut throats "just to keep their hands in", as Sallust[18] rather nicely puts it.

'So France has learnt by bitter experience how dangerous it is to keep these savage pets, but there are plenty of similar object-lessons in the history of Rome, Carthage, Syria, and many other countries. Again and again standing armies have seized some opportunity of overthrowing the government that employed them, devastating its territory, and destroying its towns. And yet it's quite unnecessary. That's obvious enough from the fact that for all their intensive military training the French can't often claim to have beaten your wartime conscripts – I won't put it more strongly than that, for fear of seeming to flatter present company.

'Besides, it's not generally thought that either of the types you mentioned, the tradesmen in town or the ignorant farmhand in the country, is actually so very frightened of the retainers in question – unless his physical strength isn't equal to his courage, or his spirit has been broken by privations at home. The fact is that though these retainers start off with powerful physiques – for no gentleman would stoop to corrupt an inferior specimen – they soon get soft and flabby by sitting around doing nothing, or nothing that a woman couldn't do. So there's really not much risk of their losing all their manhood, if they were taught useful trades and made to work like men. In any case I don't see how it can possibly be in the public interest to prepare for a war, which you needn't have unless you want to, by maintaining innumerable disturbers of the peace – when peace is so infinitely more important.

'But that's not the only thing that compels people to steal. There are other factors at work which must, I think, be peculiar to your country.'

'And what are they?' asked the Cardinal.

'Sheep,' I told him. 'These placid creatures, which used to require so little food, have now apparently developed a raging appetite, and turned into man-eaters. Fields, houses, towns, everything goes down their throats. To put it more plainly, in those parts of the kingdom where the finest, and so the most expensive wool is produced, the nobles and gentlemen, not to mention several saintly abbots, have grown dissatisfied with the income that their predecessors got out of their estates. They're no longer content to lead lazy, comfortable lives, which do no good to society – they must actively do it harm, by enclosing all the land they can for pasture, and leaving none for cultivation. They're even tearing down houses and demolishing whole towns – except, of course, for the churches, which they preserve for use as sheepfolds. As though they didn't waste enough of your soil already on their coverts and game-preserves, these kind souls have started destroying all traces of human habitation, and turning every scrap of farmland into a wilderness.

'So what happens? Each greedy individual preys on his native land like a malignant growth, absorbing field after field, and enclosing thousands of acres with a single fence. Result – hundreds of farmers are evicted. They're either cheated or bullied into giving up their property, or systematically ill-treated until they're finally forced to sell. Whichever way it's done, out the poor creatures[19] have to go, men and women, husbands and wives, widows and orphans, mothers and tiny children, together with all their employees – whose great numbers are not a sign of wealth, but simply of the fact that you can't run a farm without plenty of manpower. Out they have to go from the homes that they know so well, and they can't find anywhere else to live. Their whole stock of furniture wouldn't fetch much of a price, even if they could afford to wait for a suitable offer. But they can't, so they get very little indeed for it. By the time they've been wandering around for a bit, this little is all used up, and then what can they do but steal – and be very properly hanged? Of course, they can always become tramps and beggars, but even then they're liable to be arrested as vagrants, and put in prison for being idle – when nobody will give them a job, however much they want one. For farm-work is what they're used to, and where there's no arable land, there's no farm-work to be done. After all, it only takes one shepherd or cowherd to graze animals over an area that would need any amount of labour to make it fit for corn production.

'For the same reason, corn is much dearer in many districts. The price of wool has also risen so steeply that your poorer weavers simply can't afford to buy it, which means a lot more people thrown out of work. This is partly due to an epidemic of the rot, which destroyed vast numbers of sheep just after the conversion of arable to pasture land began. It almost looked like a judgement on the landowners for their greed – except that *they* ought to have caught it instead of the sheep.

'Not that prices would fall, however many sheep there were, for the sheep market has become, if not strictly a monopoly – for that implies only one seller – then at least an oligopoly. I mean it's almost entirely under the control of a few rich men, who don't need to sell unless they feel like it, and never do feel like it until they can get the price they want. This also accounts for the equally high prices of other types of livestock, especially in view of the shortage of breeders caused by the demolition of farms, and the general decline of agriculture. For the rich men I'm talking about never bother to breed either sheep or cattle themselves. They merely buy scraggy specimens cheap from someone else, fatten them up on their own pastures, and resell them at a large profit. I imagine that's why the full effects of the situation have not yet been felt. So far they've only inflated prices in the areas where they sell, but, if they keep transferring animals from other districts faster than they can be replaced, stocks in the buying areas too will gradually be depleted, until eventually there'll be an acute shortage everywhere.

'Thus a few greedy people have converted one of England's greatest natural advantages into a national disaster. For it's the high price of food that makes employers turn off so many of their servants – which inevitably means turning them into beggars or thieves. And theft comes easier to a man of spirit.

'To make matters worse, this wretched poverty is most incongruously linked with expensive tastes. Servants, tradesmen, even farm-labourers, in fact all classes of society are recklessly extravagant about clothes and food. Then think how many brothels there are, including those that go under the names of wine-taverns or ale-houses. Think of the demoralizing games people play – dice, cards, backgammon, tennis, bowls, quoits – what are they but quick methods of wasting a man's money, and sending him straight off to become a thief?

'Get rid of these pernicious practices. Make a law that anyone responsible for demolishing a farm or a country town must either rebuild it himself or else hand over the land to someone who's willing to do so. Stop the rich from cornering markets and establishing virtual monopolies. Reduce the number of people who are kept doing nothing. Revive agriculture and the wool industry, so that there's plenty of honest, useful work for the great army of unemployed – by which I mean not only existing thieves, but tramps and idle servants who are bound to become thieves eventually. Until you put these things right, you're not entitled to boast of the justice meted out to thieves, for it's a justice more specious than real or socially desirable. You allow these people to be brought up in the worst possible way, and systematically corrupted from their earliest years. Finally, when they grow up and commit the crimes that they were obviously destined to commit, ever since they were children, you start punishing them. In other words, you create thieves, and then punish them for stealing!'

Long before I'd finished, the lawyer was ready with his answer. He was evidently one of those people whose method of argument consists in repeating what you've said, rather than replying to it – as though having a good memory were all that mattered.

'That was a very fine effort,' he said, 'especially for a foreigner whose information is bound to be second-hand, and therefore inaccurate – as I'll very briefly demonstrate. I'll begin by running through the points you've made. Then I'll show where you've gone wrong through your ignorance of local conditions. And finally I'll refute all your arguments. Proceeding in that order, I think you've made four –'

'Just a moment,' interrupted the Cardinal. 'After such an introduction, your reply seems unlikely to be as brief as you suggest. So don't bother to produce it now – keep it fresh for your next meeting. Why not make it tomorrow, if you're both free then? Meanwhile, my dear Raphael, I'd very much like to hear just why you object to capital punishment for theft, and what penalty you think would be more in the public interest. For even you, I take it, feel that stealing should be stopped. And since it goes on merrily in spite of the death penalty, what power on earth could stop it, what possible deterrent could be effective, if the fear of death were removed? Surely any reduction of sentence would be interpreted as a positive invitation to crime?'

'Your Grace,' I said, 'it seems to me quite unjust to take a man's life because he's taken some money. To my mind no amount of property is equivalent to a human life. If it's argued that the punishment is not for taking the money, but for breaking the law and violating justice, isn't this conception of absolute justice absolutely unjust? One really can't approve of a régime so dictatorial that the slightest disobedience is punishable by death, nor of a legal code based on the Stoic paradox that all offences are equal – so that there's no distinction in law between theft and murder, though in equity the two things are so completely different.

'God said, "Thou shalt not kill" – does the theft of a little money make it quite all right for us to do so? If it's said that this commandment applies only to illegal killing, what's to prevent human beings from similarly agreeing among themselves to legalize certain types of rape, adultery, or perjury? Considering that God has forbidden us even to kill ourselves, can we really believe that purely human arrangements for the regulation of mutual slaughter are enough, without any divine authority, to exempt executioners from the sixth commandment? Isn't that rather like saying that this particular commandment has no more validity than human laws allow it? – in which case the principle can be extended indefinitely, until in all spheres of life human beings decide just how far God's commandments may conveniently be observed.

'Under the law of Moses – which was harsh enough in all conscience, being designed for slaves, and rebellious ones at that – thieves were not hanged, but merely fined. We can hardly suppose that the new dispensation, which expresses God's fatherly kindness towards His children, allows us more scope than the old for being cruel to one another.

'Well, those are my objections on moral grounds. From a practical point of view, surely it's obvious that to punish thieves and murderers in precisely the same way is not only absurd but also highly dangerous for the public. If a thief knows that a conviction for murder will get him into no more trouble than a conviction for theft, he's naturally impelled to kill the person that he'd otherwise merely have robbed. It's no worse for him if he's caught, and it gives him a better chance of not being caught, and of concealing the crime altogether by eliminating the only witness. So in our efforts to terrorize thieves we're actually encouraging them to murder innocent people.

'Now for the usual question – what punishment would be better? I'd have found it much harder to answer, if you'd asked me what would be worse. Well, why should we doubt the value of a system which those expert administrators, the Romans, found satisfactory for so long? They, as we know, sentenced people convicted of major crimes to penal servitude for life in mines or stone quarries.

'However, the best arrangement I know is one I came across while travelling through Persia, in a district generally known as Tallstoria. The Tallstorians form quite a large and well-organized community, which is completely autonomous, except for having to pay taxes to the King of Persia. As they're a long way from the sea, practically encircled by mountains, and content to live on the produce of their own soil, which is extremely fertile, they have little contact with foreigners. They've never had any wish to increase their territory, which is secured against external aggression both by the mountains and by the protection-money that they pay to the Great King. This means that they're exempt from military service, so they're able to live in comfort, if not in luxury, and be happy, if not exactly famous or glorious – for, apart from their immediate neighbours, I doubt if anyone has ever heard of them.

'Well, in Tallstoria a convicted thief has to return what he's stolen to its owner, not, as in most other countries, to the King – who according to the Tallstorians has just about as much right to it as the thief himself. If the stolen goods are no longer in his possession, their value is deducted from his own property, the rest of which is handed over intact to his wife and children. He himself is sentenced to hard labour. Except in cases of robbery with violence, he's not put in prison or made to wear fetters, but left quite free and employed on public works. If he downs tools or goes slow, they don't slow him down still more by loading him with chains – they accelerate his movements with a whip. If he works hard, he's not treated at all

badly. He has to answer a roll-call every evening, and he's
locked up for the night – but otherwise, apart from having to
work very long hours, he has a perfectly comfortable life.

'The food, for instance, is quite reasonable. It's provided at
the public expense, since convicts work as servants of the public. The procedure for raising the money varies from place to
place. In some districts it's collected from voluntary contributions. This sounds an unreliable method, but in practice it
brings in more than any other, for the people there are extraordinarily kind-hearted. Elsewhere, certain public revenues are
set aside for the purpose, or a special poll-tax is levied. There
are also some places where, instead of being employed on
public works, convicts are hired out to private enterprise.
Anyone needing their services goes to the market-place and
engages them by the day, at a rather lower wage than he would
pay for free labour. He's also allowed to whip them if they
don't work hard enough. This system ensures that they're
never out of work, their meals are provided for them, and
each convict makes a daily contribution to public funds.

'They all wear clothes of a special colour,[20] which nobody
else wears. Their heads aren't actually shaved, but the hair is
clipped short just above the ears, and a tiny piece is cut off
one of them. Their friends are allowed to give them food and
drink, and clothes of the regulation colour, but it's a capital
crime for anyone to give them money, or for them to accept
it. So it is for free men to accept money on any pretext from
slaves – as convicts are usually called – or for slaves to touch
any kind of weapon.

'Each slave is given a badge to show which district he
belongs to, and it's a capital crime to take one's badge off, to
be seen outside one's own district, or to speak to a slave from
another district. As for running away, it's just as risky to plan
it as to do it. The penalty for being accessory to any such plan
is death for a slave, and slavery for a free man – whereas by
betraying an escape-project you can earn a reward in cash, if
you're a free man, or your freedom, if you're a slave. In either
case the informer receives a pardon for his part in the plot, on
the principle that it must always be safer to abandon a criminal
undertaking than to go ahead with it.

'Well, that's how the system works, and it's obviously most convenient and humane. It comes down heavily on crime, but it saves the lives of criminals, treating them in such a way that they're forced to become good citizens, and spend the rest of their lives making up for the harm they've done in the past.

'In fact there's so little risk of their relapsing into their old habits, that they're generally regarded as the safest possible guides for long-distance travellers, who employ them in relays, one for each district they pass through. You see, slaves have no facilities for highway-robbery. They're not allowed to carry weapons. If money is found on them, it proves that they've committed a crime. If they're caught, punishment is automatic, and they haven't the slightest hope of not being caught – for how can you make an unobtrusive getaway when your clothes are quite different from ordinary people's, unless you decamp in the nude? – and even then your ear will betray you.

'There's still, of course, a theoretical risk that they might start a conspiracy to overthrow the government. But how could the slaves of any one district hope to organize such a large-scale operation, without first sounding and stirring up the slaves in several other districts? And that's physically impossible. They're not even allowed to meet them, or talk to them, or say good morning to them, let alone conspire with them. Besides, can you imagine anyone cheerfully letting the other slaves of his district into a secret which would be so dangerous for them to keep, and so very profitable for them to betray? On the other hand, every slave has some hope of recovering his freedom, simply by doing what he's told and giving the authorities reason to believe that he'll go straight in future – since a certain number of slaves are released every year for good conduct.'

I then added that I didn't see why this system shouldn't be adopted in England. It would produce far better results than the so-called 'justice' that the lawyer had praised so highly.

At this our learned friend – I mean the lawyer – shook his head.

'Such a system,' he announced, with a smile of contempt,

'could never be adopted in England, without serious danger to the country.'

That was all he said – and practically everyone else agreed with him.

Then the Cardinal gave his opinion.

'It's hard to predict,' he said, 'without giving it a trial, whether it would work or not. But suppose the King were to postpone the execution of death sentences for an experimental period – having first abolished all rights of asylum. If the results were good, we'd be justified in making the arrangement permanent. If not, the original sentences could still be carried out, with quite as much benefit to society, and quite as much justice, as if they were carried out now. In the meantime no great harm could have been done. As a matter of fact, I don't think it would be at all a bad idea to treat vagrants in the same way. We're always making laws about them, but so far nothing has had the slightest effect.'

This, from the Cardinal, was enough to make everyone wildly in favour of an idea which nobody had taken seriously when *I* produced it. They were particularly keen on the bit about vagrants, since that was his own contribution.

Perhaps I ought to leave out the next part of the conversation, which was not wholly serious. But I don't think I shall, because it was perfectly harmless, and had a certain relevance to the point at issue. Among those present was a professional diner-out, who wanted you to think that he was merely acting the fool but played the part almost too convincingly. His efforts to raise a laugh were usually so feeble that one tended to laugh at him rather than with him. But occasionally he'd come out with something rather good, thus restoring one's faith in the proverb, 'If at first you don't succeed, try, try, try again.' Well, somebody gave him his cue by remarking that the Cardinal and I between us had solved the problem of thieves and vagrants, so it only remained to decide on appropriate state action to deal with poor people who were either too old or too ill to earn their living.

'Just leave it to me,' said this gentleman. 'I'll tell you exactly what to do. The fact is, I'm desperately anxious to get that sort of person out of my sight. I've suffered so often from demands for money in that whining sing-song of theirs – a form of music which has never charmed a penny out of me. What always happens is this – either I don't feel like giving them anything, or else I do, but I can't, because I haven't got anything to give. So now they're learning not to waste their energy. When they see me walking past, they just *let* me walk past, without saying a word. They know I might as well be a priest, for all the help I'll be to them. Well, I propose a law for the compulsory enrolment of beggars in Benedictine monasteries, the males to become lay brethren – that's the technical term for monks – and the females to become nuns.'

The Cardinal smiled, and jokingly agreed. So did all the others, with perfectly straight faces. The only exception was a certain friar, who'd apparently studied theology. Normally a grimly serious type of person, he was so delighted by these digs at priests and monks that he too started trying to be funny.

'Ah, but you won't get rid of beggars quite so easily,' he said. 'What are you going to do about us mendicant friars?'

'Why, that's already taken care of,' replied the wag. 'Don't you remember the Cardinal's splendid regulation for the control and useful employment of tramps?'

Everyone glanced at the Cardinal, to see how he was taking it, and, as he showed no signs of disapproval, the remark was greeted with applause – except by the friar. He, not very surprisingly, reacted to this cold douche of satire by losing his temper and becoming downright abusive. He called the man every rude name he could think of, including a son of Belial, and wound up with some fearful curses out of Holy Scripture.

At this point the clown started clowning in real earnest. He obviously felt in his element.

'My dear friar,' he began, 'you mustn't get so angry. You know what it says in the Bible, "Ye shall possess your souls in patience".'[21]

'I'm not angry, damn you!' shouted the friar – those were his very words. 'Or if I am, I've every right to be. "Be ye angry, and sin not",[22] that's what it says in the Psalms.'

The Cardinal gently suggested that he should try to keep his temper.

'My temper, sir?' he repeated. 'There's nothing wrong with

my temper. It's righteous zeal that makes me say these things, the sort of righteous zeal that inspired the saints. Hence the words of the Psalmist, "The zeal of thy house hath eaten me up",[23] or of the hymn that we sing in church:

> They who mocked the great Elisha,
> As he mounted up to Bethel,
> By a baldhead's zeal was punished.[24].

And I dare say this filthy sneering idiot may find the same thing happening to him.'

'I'm sure your feelings do you great credit,' said the Cardinal, 'but I wonder if your behaviour wouldn't be even more saintly – it would certainly be wiser – if you refrained from making a fool of yourself by arguing with a fool.'

'No, sir,' retorted the friar, 'it would not be wiser, for who could be wiser than Solomon? And Solomon says, "Answer a fool according to his folly"[25] – which is precisely what I'm doing. I'm showing him the bottomless pit that he's liable to fall into, if he isn't very careful. In Elisha's case, it was forty-two mockers against only one baldhead, and yet his zeal was enough to punish them. So how much worse it's going to be for this man here – a single mocker against all the friars in Christendom, a very high proportion of whom are bald! Besides, we have a Papal Bull expressly forbidding anyone to mock us, on pain of excommunication.'

Seeing that the thing would go on indefinitely, the Cardinal gave the wit a sign to withdraw, and tactfully changed the subject. A few minutes later he got up and dismissed us, as he had to interview some people who'd applied to him for help.

Well, my dear More, I'm afraid I've subjected you to a very long lecture. Only you really did ask for it – and you listened so attentively that I felt you wouldn't want me to leave anything out. Anyway, the conversation seemed worth repeating, if only in general outline, so as to give you some idea of the way these people think. You see, everything I said was treated with contempt, until it appeared that the Cardinal was not against it – and then they were immediately all for it. In their efforts to flatter him, they were even prepared to applaud, and almost take seriously the suggestions made by a hanger-on of his, simply because the great man laughingly approved of them. So you can guess how much notice people would take of me and my advice at Court!

MORE: My dear Raphael, I enjoyed every word of it. There's so much wit and wisdom in everything you say. Besides, it all carried me back, not merely to England, but in a sense to my own boyhood – it recalled such pleasant memories of the Cardinal, in whose household I was brought up. I liked you from the start, my dear Raphael, but you've no idea how much your warm tribute to his memory has increased my feeling for you. But I still can't help thinking that if you could only overcome your aversion to court life, your advice would be extremely useful to the public. Which means that it's your positive duty, as a good man, to give it. You know what your friend Plato says[26] – that a happy state of society will never be achieved, until philosophers are kings, or kings take to studying philosophy. Well, just think how infinitely remote that happy state must remain, if philosophers won't even condescend to give kings a word of advice!

RAPHAEL: Oh, philosophers aren't as bad as all that. They'd be only too glad to offer advice – in fact many of them have done so already in their published works – if only people in power would listen to them. And that's doubtless what Plato meant. He realized that kings are too deeply infected with wrong ideas in childhood to take any philosopher's advice, unless they become philosophers themselves – as he learned by experience with Dionysius.[27] What do you suppose would happen if I started telling a king to make sensible laws, or trying to expel the deadly germs of bad ones from his mind? I'd be promptly thrown out, or merely treated as a figure of fun.

For instance, just imagine me in France, at a top-secret meeting of the Cabinet. The King himself is in the chair, and round the table sit all his expert advisers, earnestly discussing ways and means of solving the following problems:[28] how can His Majesty keep a grip on Milan, and get Naples back into his clutches? How can he conquer Venice, and complete the subjection of Italy? How can he then establish control over Flanders, Brabant, and finally the whole of Burgundy? – not to mention all the other countries that he has already invaded in his dreams.

One gentleman proposes a pact with the Venetians, to remain in force for just so long as the King shall find convenient. He should take them into his confidence, and even allow them a certain amount of the plunder – he can always demand it back later, when he has got what he wants. Another gentleman recommends the employment of German mercenaries, and a third is in favour of greasing the palms of the Swiss. A fourth advises His Majesty to propitiate the Holy Roman Empire with a sacrifice of gold. A fifth thinks it might be wise for him to improve relations with the King of Aragon, and as a peace-offering hand over the kingdom of Navarre[29] – which doesn't belong to him anyway. Meanwhile a sixth is proposing that the Prince of Castile should be enticed into the French camp by promises of a marriage alliance, and that some of his courtiers should be paid a regular salary for their support.

And now for the knottiest problem of all – what's to be done about the English? Well, obviously the first step is to arrange a peace-conference, and conclude a solemn treaty of alliance which means absolutely nothing. In other words, call them friends, but regard them as potential enemies. The Scotch must therefore be kept standing by, ready to start an invasion at a moment's notice, in case the English make the slightest move. It might also be as well to offer secret encouragement – under the terms of the treaty it can't be done openly – to some exiled English nobleman[30] with pretensions to the throne. This would give His Majesty an extra hold over the King of England, whom he otherwise wouldn't trust an inch.

At this point, while all these mighty forces are being set in motion, and all these worthy gentlemen are producing rival plans of campaign, up gets little Raphael, and proposes a complete reversal of policy. I advise the King to forget about Italy and stay at home. I tell him that France is already almost too big for one man to govern properly, so he really needn't worry about acquiring extra territory.

I then refer to an incident in the history of Nolandia, a country just south-east of Utopia. On the strength of some ancient marriage, the King of Nolandia thought he had a

hereditary claim to another kingdom, so his people started a
war to get it for him. Eventually they won, only to find that
the kingdom in question was quite as much trouble to keep
as it had been to acquire. There were constant threats of internal
rebellion and external aggression. They were always having to
fight either for their new subjects or against them. They never
got a chance to demobilize, and in the meantime they were being
ruined. All their money was going out of the country, and men
were losing their lives to pay for someone else's petty ambition.
Conditions at home were no safer than they'd been during the
war, which had lowered moral standards, by encouraging
people to kill and steal. There was no respect whatever for the
law, because the king's attention was divided between the two
kingdoms, so that he couldn't concentrate properly on either.

Seeing that this hopeless situation would continue indefinitely, if they didn't do something about it, the Nolandians
finally decided on a course of action, which was to ask the king,
quite politely, which kingdom he wanted to keep.

'You can't keep them both,' they explained, 'because there
are too many of us to be governed by half a king. Why, even
if we were a lot of mules, it would be a full-time job looking
after us!'

So that exemplary monarch was forced to hand over the new
kingdom to a friend of his – who was very soon thrown out –
and make do with the old one.

I also remind the French King that even if he does start all
these wars and create chaos in all these different countries, he's
still quite liable to find in the end that he has ruined himself
and destroyed his people for nothing. I therefore advise him
to concentrate on the kingdom that his ancestors handed down
to him, and make it as beautiful and as prosperous as he can, to
love his own subjects and deserve their love, to live among
them and govern them kindly, and to give up all ideas of
territorial expansion, because he has got more than enough to
deal with already.

Now tell me, my dear More, how do you think he'll react
to my advice?

MORE: Not terribly well, I must admit.

RAPHAEL: Now let's imagine another situation. Suppose

some king's financial advisers are discussing how to increase his capital. One suggests raising the value of the currency[31] when the King has to pay money out, and lowering it abnormally when payments are due to him. This will have the effect of increasing his receipts, and reducing the cost of meeting his liabilities. A second suggests that the King should pretend to start a war.[32] This will give him an excuse for levying extra taxes. Then, at his own convenience, he can solemnly make peace, while posing, for the benefit of the lower orders, as a kind ruler who can't bear the thought of bloodshed. A third reminds him of some moth-eaten old law, which has long been obsolete – which everybody breaks, because nobody's aware of its existence – and urges him to collect the fines so incurred. It will greatly redound to his credit, in a moral as well as a financial sense – for the operation will be carried out under the cloak of justice. A fourth[33] advises him to introduce legislation imposing heavy fines for certain offences, preferably of the most anti-social type. He can then sell exemption from such laws to anyone who finds them inconvenient. This will ensure his popularity with the general public, while providing a double source of revenue – for first he'll get the fines collected from profiteers who fall into his trap, and secondly he'll get the money paid for special dispensations. Of course, the price of these will vary in proportion to the King's moral character. The higher his principles, the more reluctant he'll be to let anyone act against the public interest – so the more a dispensation will cost.

A fifth recommends him to get some hold over the judges, so that they'll always give a verdict in his favour. He should also invite them to the Palace, and consult them about his legal position. He may be quite obviously in the wrong, but one of the judges is sure to discover a loophole which will serve to defeat justice. Whatever motives he may have for doing so – a passion for contradiction, a dislike of the obvious, or a simple wish to please – the result will be the same. Soon every judge will be voicing a different opinion, a perfectly clear case will begin to seem controversial, and the plainest facts will be questioned. This will give the King a splendid chance of interpreting the law to his own advantage. Everyone else will agree, from either fear or politeness, and eventually this interpretation will be boldly pronounced from the Bench. After all, there are so many ways of justifying a verdict for the Crown. One can either appeal to equity, or to the letter of the law, or to some perversion of its meaning, or in the last resort to a principle which carries more weight with conscientious judges than any law on earth – the 'indisputable royal prerogative'.

There's unanimous support for the doctrine of Crassus,[34] that you can never have enough money, if you've got an army to maintain. It's also generally agreed that a King can do no wrong, however much he may want to, because everything belongs to him, including every human being in the country, and private property does not exist, except in so far as he's kind enough not to seize it.[35] He should always reduce such provisional private property to a minimum, since his safety depends on preventing his subjects from having too much wealth or freedom. These things make people less willing to put up with injustice and oppression, whereas poverty and privation make them dull and submissive, and stifle the noble spirit of rebellion.

At this point I get up again, and say that it would be most unwise as well as most immoral for the King to do any of these things, because his prestige and security depend less on his own than on his subjects' wealth.

'Why do you suppose they made you king in the first place?' I ask him. 'Not for your benefit, but for theirs. They meant you to devote your energies to making their lives more comfortable, and protecting them from injustice. So your job is to see that they're all right, not that you are – just as a shepherd's job, strictly speaking, is to feed his sheep, not himself. As for the theory that peace is best preserved by keeping the people poor, it's completely contradicted by the facts. Beggars are far the most quarrelsome section of the community. Who is more likely to start a revolution than a man who's discontented with his present living conditions? Who could have a stronger impulse to turn everything upside down in the hope of personal profit, than a man who'd got nothing to lose?

'No, if a king is so hated or despised by his subjects that he can't keep them in order unless he reduces them to beggary by violence, extortion, and confiscation, he'd far better abdicate. Such methods of staying in power may preserve the title, but they destroy the majesty of a king. There's nothing majestic about ruling a nation of beggars – true majesty consists in governing the rich and prosperous. That's what that admirable character Fabricius[36] meant when he said he'd rather govern rich men than be one. Certainly a man who enjoys a life of luxury while everyone else is moaning and groaning round him can hardly be called a king – he's more like a gaoler.

'In short, it's a pretty poor doctor who can't cure one disease without giving you another, and a king who can't suppress crime without lowering standards of living should admit that he just doesn't know how to govern free men. He should start by suppressing one of his own vices – either his pride or his laziness, for those are the faults most liable to make a king hated or despised. He should live on his own resources, without being a nuisance to others. He should adapt his expenditure to his income. He should prevent crime by sound administration rather than allow it to develop and then start punishing it. He should hesitate to enforce any law which has long been disregarded – especially if people have got on perfectly well without it. And he should never invent a crime as an excuse for imposing a fine – no private person would be allowed to do anything so dishonest.'

I then proceed to tell them about a system they have in Happiland, a country not far from Utopia. There the King has to swear a solemn oath at his coronation that he'll never keep more than a thousand pounds of gold in his treasury, or an equivalent amount of silver. Apparently the system was started by an excellent king of theirs, who cared more about his country's welfare than his own. He thought it would prevent the accumulation of royal wealth on such a scale as to cause national poverty, and chose that particular figure because he reckoned it would be enough to suppress a revolution or repel an invasion, but not enough to inspire a king with thoughts of foreign conquest. That was his main idea, but not his only one. He also hoped this arrangement would ensure that there was always enough money in circulation for ordinary purposes of exchange, and that the King would have no motive for raising money unfairly, since he wouldn't be allowed to keep any capital in excess of the statutory limit. Now there you have the type of king who's feared by bad men and loved by good ones – but if I said things like that to people who were quite determined to take the opposite view, do you think they'd listen to me?

MORE: Of course they wouldn't, and I can't say I'd blame them. Frankly, I don't see the point of saying things like that, or of giving advice that you know they'll never accept. What possible good could it do? How can they be expected to take in a totally unfamiliar line of thought, which goes against all their deepest prejudices? That sort of thing is quite fun in a friendly conversation, but at a Cabinet meeting, where major decisions of policy have to be made, such philosophizing would be completely out of place.

RAPHAEL: That's exactly what I was saying – there's no room at Court for philosophy.

MORE: There's certainly no room for the academic variety, which says what it thinks irrespective of circumstances. But there is a more civilized form of philosophy which knows the dramatic context, so to speak, tries to fit in with it, and plays an appropriate part in the current performance. That's the sort you should go in for. Otherwise it would be like interrupting some comedy[37] by Plautus, in which a lot of slaves were fooling about, by rushing on to the stage dressed up as a philosopher, and spouting a bit of that scene in the *Octavia*[38] where Seneca is arguing with Nero. Surely it would be better to keep your mouth shut altogether than to turn the thing into a tragicomedy by interpolating lines from a different play? For, even if your contribution were an improvement on what had gone before, the effect would be so incongruous that you'd ruin the whole show. No, do the best you can to make the present production a success – don't spoil the entire play just because you happen to think of another one that you'd enjoy rather more.

The same rule applies to politics and life at Court. If you can't completely eradicate wrong ideas, or deal with inveterate vices as effectively as you could wish, that's no reason for turning your back on public life altogether. You wouldn't abandon ship in a storm just because you couldn't control the winds.

On the other hand, it's no use attempting to put across entirely new ideas, which will obviously carry no weight with people who are prejudiced against them. You must go to work indirectly. You must handle everything as tactfully as you can, and what you can't put right you must try to make as little wrong as possible. For things will never be perfect, until human beings are perfect – which I don't expect them to be for quite a number of years!

RAPHAEL: The only advantage of that method would be that I mightn't find it quite so maddening as making a real effort to cure other people's madness. But if I'm to speak the truth, I'll have to say the sort of things that you object to. I don't know whether it's right for a philosopher to tell lies, but it's certainly not my way. Besides, though they might be annoyed by what I said, I don't see why it should be thought so fantastically out of the ordinary. It's not as if I'd recommended the system operated in Plato's imaginary *Republic*, or in Utopia today. Now that, while undoubtedly better than ours, might well strike them as rather odd, because it's based on communal ownership instead of private property.

Of course they wouldn't like my proposals. Having set their hearts on a certain course of action, they'd naturally resent being shown the dangers that lay ahead, and told to give the whole thing up. But apart from that, what did I say that couldn't or shouldn't be said in any company? If we're never to say anything that might be thought unconventional, for fear of its sounding ridiculous, we'll have to hush up, even in a Christian country, practically everything that Christ taught. But that was the last thing He wanted. Didn't He tell His disciples that everything He had whispered in their ears should be proclaimed on the housetops?[39] And most of His teaching is far more at variance with modern conventions than anything I suggested, except in so far as His doctrines have been modified by ingenious preachers – doubtless on your recommendation!

'We'll never get human behaviour in line with Christian ethics,' these gentlemen must have argued, 'so let's adapt Christian ethics to human behaviour. Then at least there'll be some connexion between them.'

But I can't see what good they've done. They've merely enabled people to sin with a clear conscience – and that's about all I could do at a Cabinet meeting. For I'd either have to vote against my colleagues, which would be equivalent to not voting at all, or else I'd have to vote with them, in which case, like Micio in Terence,[40] I'd be 'aiding and abetting insanity'.

As for working indirectly, and when things can't be put right, handling them so tactfully that they're as little wrong as possible, I don't quite see what that means. At Court you can't keep your opinions to yourself, or merely connive at other people's crimes. You have to give open support to deplorable policies, and subscribe to utterly monstrous resolutions. If you don't show enough enthusiasm for a bad law, you'll be taken for a spy or even a traitor. Besides, what chance have you got of doing any good, when you're working with colleagues like that? You'll never reform them – they're far more likely to corrupt you, however admirable a character you are. By associating with them you'll either lose your own integrity, or else have it used to conceal their folly and wickedness. So much for the practical results of your indirect method!

There's a delightful image in Plato,[41] which explains why a sensible person is right to steer clear of politics. He sees everyone else rushing into the street and getting soaked in the pouring rain. He can't persuade them to go indoors and keep dry. He knows if he went out too, he'd merely get equally wet. So he just stays indoors himself, and, as he can't do anything about other people's stupidity, comforts himself with the thought: 'Well, I'm all right, anyway.'

Though, to tell you the truth, my dear More, I don't see how you can ever get any real justice or prosperity, so long as there's private property, and everything's judged in terms of money – unless you consider it just for the worst sort of people to have the best living conditions, or unless you're prepared to call a country prosperous, in which all the wealth is owned by a tiny minority – who aren't entirely happy even so, while everyone else is simply miserable.

In fact, when I think of the fair and sensible arrangements in Utopia, where things are run so efficiently with so few laws, and recognition of individual merit is combined with equal prosperity for all – when I compare Utopia with a great many capitalist countries which are always making new regulations, but could never be called well-regulated, where dozens of laws are passed every day, and yet there are still not enough to ensure that one can either earn, or keep, or safely identify one's so-called private property – or why such an endless succession of never-ending lawsuits? – when I consider all this, I feel much more sympathy with Plato, and much less surprise at his refusal to legislate for a city[42] that rejected egalitarian principles. It was evidently quite obvious to a powerful intellect like his that the one essential condition for a healthy society was equal distribution of goods – which I suspect is impossible under capitalism. For, when everyone's entitled to get as much for himself as he can, all available property, however much there is of it, is bound to fall into the hands of a small minority, which means that everyone else is poor. And wealth will tend to vary in inverse proportion to merit. The rich will be greedy, unscrupulous, and totally useless characters, while the poor will be simple, unassuming people whose daily work is far more profitable to the community than it is to them.

In other words, I'm quite convinced that you'll never get a fair distribution of goods, or a satisfactory organization of human life, until you abolish private property altogether. So long as it exists, the vast majority of the human race, and the vastly superior part of it, will inevitably go on labouring under a burden of poverty, hardship, and worry. I don't say that the burden can't be reduced, but you'll never take it right off their shoulders. You might, of course, set a statutory limit to the amount of money or land that any one person is allowed to possess. You might, by suitable legislation, maintain a balance of power between the King and his subjects. You might make it illegal to buy, or even to apply for a public appointment, and unnecessary for a state official to spend any money of his own – otherwise he's liable to recoup his losses by fraud and extortion, and wealth, rather than wisdom, becomes the essential qualification for such posts. Laws of that type would certainly relieve the symptoms, just as a chronic invalid gets some benefit from constant medical attention. But there's no hope of a cure, so long as private property continues. If you try to treat an outbreak in one part of the body politic, you merely exacerbate the symptoms elsewhere. What's medicine for some people is poison for others – because you can never pay Paul without robbing Peter.

MORE: I disagree. I don't believe you'd ever have a reasonable standard of living under a communist system. There'd always tend to be shortages, because nobody would work hard enough. In the absence of a profit motive, everyone would become lazy, and rely on everyone else to do the work for him. Then, when things really got short, the inevitable result would be a series of murders and riots, since nobody would have any legal method of protecting the products of his own labour – especially as there wouldn't be any respect for authority, or I don't see how there could be, in a classless society.

RAPHAEL: You're bound to take that view, for you simply can't imagine what it would be like – not accurately, at any rate. But if you'd been with me in Utopia, and seen it all for yourself, as I did – I lived there for more than five years, you know, and the only reason why I ever left was that I wanted to tell people about the New World – you'd be the first to admit that you'd never seen a country so well organized.

PETER: I must say, I find it hard to believe that things are so much better organized in the New World than in the Old. I should think we're just as intelligent as they are, and our civilization is older. It therefore embodies the fruits of long experience, by which I mean all the schemes that we've worked out for making life more comfortable – not to mention several chance discoveries, which could never have been achieved by deliberate planning.

RAPHAEL: You'd be more qualified to judge the age of their civilization, if you'd read their history books. If these are to be trusted, there were towns in the New World before human life had even begun in the Old. As for what you say about intelligence and chance discoveries, there's no reason to suppose we have a monopoly of either. We may or may not be more intelligent than they are, but I'm quite sure they leave us far behind in their capacity for concentration and hard work. According to their records, they'd had no contact whatsoever with Transequatorials, as they call us, until we landed there –

except on one occasion, twelve hundred years ago, when a ship was driven off its course in a storm, and wrecked on the coast of Utopia. A few survivors managed to swim ashore, including some Romans and Egyptians, who settled there for good.

Now, this will give you some idea what good use they make of their opportunities. There wasn't a single useful technique practised anywhere in the Roman Empire that they didn't either learn from these survivors, or else work out for themselves, once they'd been given the first clue. They got all that from just one contact with our hemisphere. But if, by any similar accident, a Utopian has ever found his way over here, we've completely forgotten about it, as I dare say people will soon forget that I was ever there. On the strength of our first meeting, they immediately adopted all the best ideas that Europe has produced – but I doubt if we'd be quite so quick to take over any of their arrangements which are better than ours. And that's the main reason, I think, why although they've got no more intelligence or natural resources than we have, they're so much ahead of us politically and economically.

MORE: In that case, my dear Raphael, for goodness' sake tell us some more about the island in question. Don't try to be too concise – give us a detailed account of it from every point of view, geographical, sociological, political, legal – in fact, tell us everything you think we'd like to know, which means everything we don't know already.

RAPHAEL: There's nothing I'd enjoy more, for it's all quite fresh in my memory. But it'll take some time, you understand.

MORE: All right, let's go in to lunch straight away. Then we'll have the whole afternoon at our disposal.

RAPHAEL: Let's do just that.

So we went indoors and had lunch. After the meal we returned to the same spot, sat down on the same bench, and told the servants we were not to be disturbed. Then Peter Gilles and I asked Raphael to keep his promise. Seeing that we really meant it, he took a few moments to collect his thoughts, and then began as follows:

BOOK TWO

RAPHAEL: Well, the island is broadest in the middle, where it measures about two hundred miles across. It's never much narrower than that, except towards the very ends, which gradually taper away and curve right round, just as if they'd been drawn with a pair of compasses, until they almost form a circle five hundred miles in circumference. So you can picture the island as a sort of crescent,[1] with its tips divided by a strait approximately eleven miles wide. Through this the sea flows in, and then spreads out into an enormous lake – though it really looks more like a vast standing pool, for, as it's completely protected from the wind by the surrounding land, the water never gets rough. Thus practically the whole interior of the island serves as a harbour, and boats can sail across it in all directions, which is very useful for everyone.

The harbour mouth is alarmingly full of rocks and shoals. One of these rocks presents no danger to shipping, for it rises high out of the water, almost in the middle of the gap, and has a tower built on it, which is permanently garrisoned. But the other rocks are deadly, because you can't see them. Only the Utopians know where the safe channels are, so without a Utopian pilot it's practically impossible for a foreign ship to enter the harbour. It would be risky enough even for the local inhabitants, if it weren't for certain landmarks erected on the shore – and by simply shifting these landmarks they could lure any number of enemy warships to destruction. Of course, there are plenty of harbours on the other side of the island, but they're all so well fortified, either naturally or artificially, that a handful of men could easily prevent a huge invading force from landing at any of them.

They say, though, and one can actually see for oneself, that Utopia was originally not an island but a peninsula. However, it was conquered by somebody called Utopos, who gave it its present name – it used to be called Sansculottia – and was also responsible for transforming a pack of ignorant savages into what is now, perhaps, the most civilized nation in the world. The moment he landed and got control of the country, he immediately had a channel cut through the fifteen-mile isthmus connecting Utopia with the mainland, so that the sea could flow all round it. Fearing it might cause resentment if he made the local inhabitants do all the work, he put his whole army on the job as well. With this colossal labour force, he got it done incredibly quickly, to the great surprise and terror of the people on the mainland, who'd begun by making fun of the whole idea.

There are fifty-four splendid big towns on the island, all with the same language, laws, customs, and institutions. They're all built on the same plan, and, so far as the sites will allow, they all look exactly alike. The minimum distance between towns is twenty-four miles, and the maximum, no more than a day's walk.

Each town sends three of its older and more experienced citizens to an annual meeting at Aircastle, to discuss the general affairs of the island. Aircastle is regarded as the capital, because of its central position, which makes it easy to get at from every part of the country. The distribution of land is so arranged that the territory of each town stretches for at least twenty miles in every direction, and in one direction much farther – that is, where the distance between towns reaches its maximum. No town has the slightest wish to extend its boundaries, for they don't regard their land as property but as soil that they've got to cultivate.

At regular intervals all over the countryside there are houses supplied with agricultural equipment, and town dwellers take it in turns to go and live in them. Each house accommodates at least forty adults, plus two slaves who are permanently attached to it, and is run by a reliable, elderly married couple, under the supervision of a District Controller, who's responsible for thirty such houses. Each year twenty people from each house go back to town, having done two years in the country, and are replaced by twenty others. These new recruits are then taught farming by the ones who've had a year on the land already, and so know more about the job. Twelve months later the trainees become the instructors, and so on. This system reduces the risk of food shortages, which might occur if the whole agricultural population were equally inexperienced.

Two years is the normal period of work on the land, so that no one's forced to rough it for too long, but those who enjoy country life – and many people do – can get special permission to stay there longer. Landworkers are responsible for cultivating the soil, raising livestock, felling timber, and transporting it to the towns, either by land or sea, whichever is more convenient. They breed vast numbers of chickens by a most extraordinary method.[2] Instead of leaving the hens to sit on the eggs, they hatch out dozens at a time by applying a steady heat to them – with the result that, when the chicks come out of the shells, they regard the poultryman as their mother, and follow him everywhere!

They keep very few horses, and no really tame ones, as they only use them for riding practice. Ploughing and pulling carts is done by oxen. Admittedly they can't go as fast as horses, but the Utopians say they're tougher and subject to fewer diseases. They're also less trouble and less expensive to feed, and, when they're finally past work, they're still useful as meat.

Corn is used solely for making bread, for they drink no beer, only wine, cider, perry, or water – sometimes by itself, but often flavoured with honey or liquorice, which are both very plentiful. The authorities of each town work out very accurately the annual food consumption of their whole area, but they always grow corn and breed livestock far in excess of their own requirements, so that they've plenty to spare for their neighbours.

Any necessary equipment which is not available in the country is got from one's home town – for there's a holiday once a month, when most people go there. You simply ask an official for what you want, and he hands it over, without any sort of payment.

Just before harvest-time District Controllers notify the urban authorities how much extra labour they'll need. So exactly that number of harvesters turns up punctually on the right day, and, if the weather's good, gets the whole job done in something like twenty-four hours.

But I must tell you some more about the towns. Well, when you've seen one of them, you've seen them all, for they're as nearly identical as local conditions will permit. So I'll just give you one example – it doesn't much matter which. However, the obvious choice is Aircastle, for the fact that Parliament meets there gives it a special importance, and it's the one I know best, having lived there for five years.

Aircastle is built on a gently sloping hill-side, and its ground-plan is practically square. It stretches from just below the top of the hill to the River Nowater, two miles away, and extends for two miles and a bit along the river-bank.

The source of the Nowater is quite a small spring eighty miles further inland, but it's joined by several tributaries, two of them pretty big ones, so by the time it gets to Aircastle it's already more than fifty yards wide. It then keeps on growing wider, until it reaches the sea sixty miles away. Right up to the town, and for several miles beyond it, there are strong tidal currents which change direction every six hours. At high tide the sea comes thirty miles inland, filling the whole river-bed and forcing the river back. The water turns brackish for some distance further up-stream, but after that the taste of salt gradually disappears, and the water which flows past Aircastle is absolutely fresh. At low tide the river chases the sea back, and continues pure and uncontaminated practically all the way to the coast.

The town is connected with the other bank of the river by a splendid arched bridge, with stone piers – not just wooden ones. That's at the landward end, so that ships can have unobstructed access to one whole side of the town. There's also another river, not very big, but delightfully calm and peaceful. It gushes out of the hill on which Aircastle is built, and flows down through the middle of it to join the Nowater. The fountain-head is just outside the town, but they've brought it within the circuit of the city wall, so that in case of invasion the enemy couldn't either cut off, divert, or poison their water supply. From that point water is run off to the lower districts of the town through a system of brickwork pipes. Where this method won't work, they have huge cisterns to collect rain-water – which serves the purpose equally well.

The town is surrounded by a thick, high wall, with towers and blockhouses at frequent intervals. On three sides of it there's also a moat, which contains no water, but is very broad

and deep, and obstructed by a thorn-bush entanglement. On
the fourth side the river serves as a moat. The streets are well
designed, both for traffic and for protection against the wind.
The buildings are far from unimpressive, for they take the
form of terraces, facing one another and running the whole
length of the street. The fronts of the houses are separated
by a twenty-foot carriageway. Behind them is a large garden,
also as long as the street itself, and completely enclosed by the
backs of other streets. Each house has a front door leading into
the street, and a back door into the garden. In both cases they're
double swing-doors, which open at a touch, and close automatically behind you. So anyone can go in and out – for there's
no such thing as private property. The houses themselves are
allocated by lot, and changed round every ten years.

They're extremely fond of these gardens, in which they grow
fruit, including grapes, as well as grass and flowers. They keep
them in wonderful condition – in fact, I've never seen anything
to beat them for beauty or fertility. The people of Aircastle
are keen gardeners not only because they enjoy it, but because
there are inter-street competitions for the best-kept garden.
Certainly it would be hard to find any feature of the town more
calculated to give pleasure and profit to the community – which
makes me think that gardening must have been one of the
founder's special interests.

By the founder I mean Utopos himself, who is said to have
designed the whole layout of the town right from the start.
However, he left posterity to embellish it and add the finishing
touches, which he realized would take more than a single
lifetime. According to their historical records, which cover a
period of 1,760 years from the Conquest, and have always
been most carefully written up, the original houses were merely
small huts or cottages, built hurriedly with the first timber that
came to hand. The walls were plastered with mud, the roofs
ridged and thatched. But nowadays every house is an imposing
three-storey structure. The walls are faced with flint or some
other hard stone, or else with bricks, and lined with roughcast.
The sloping roofs have been raised to the horizontal, and
covered with a special sort of concrete which costs next to
nothing, but is better than lead for resisting bad weather

conditions, and is also fireproof. They keep out draughts by glazing the windows – oh yes, they use a great deal of glass there – or sometimes by fitting screens of fine linen treated with clear oil or amber, which has the effect of making it more transparent and also more airtight.

Now for their system of local government. The population is divided into groups of thirty households, each of which elects an official called a Styward every year. Styward is the Old Utopian title – the modern one is District Controller. For every ten Stywards and the households they represent there is a Bencheater, or Senior District Controller.

Each town has two hundred Stywards, who are responsible for electing the Mayor.[3] They do it by secret ballot, after solemnly swearing to vote for the man that they consider best qualified. He has to be one of four candidates nominated by the whole electorate – for each quarter of the town chooses its own candidate and submits his name to the Council of Bencheaters. The Mayor remains in office for life, unless he's suspected of wanting to establish a dictatorship. Bencheaters are elected annually, but they're not normally changed. All other municipal appointments are for one year only.

Every three days, or more often if necessary, the Bencheaters have a meeting with the Mayor, at which they discuss public affairs, and promptly settle any private disputes – though these are very rare. They always invite two Stywards, a different pair each day, to attend their meetings, and there's a rule that no question affecting the general public may be finally decided until it has been debated for three days. It's a capital crime to discuss such questions anywhere except in the Council or the Assembly. Apparently this is to discourage the Mayor and Bencheaters from plotting to override the people's wishes and change the constitution. For the same reason any major issue is referred to the Assembly of Stywards, who explain it to all their households, talk it over among themselves, and then report their views to the Council. Occasionally the matter is referred to Parliament.

There's also a rule in the Council that no resolution can be debated on the day that it's first proposed. All discussion is postponed until the next well-attended meeting. Otherwise someone's liable to say the first thing that comes into his head, and then start thinking up arguments to justify what he has said, instead of trying to decide what's best for the community. That type of person is quite prepared to sacrifice the public to his own prestige, just because, absurd as it may sound, he's ashamed to admit that his first idea might have been wrong – when his first idea *should* have been to think before he spoke.

And now for their working conditions. Well, there's one job they all do, irrespective of sex, and that's farming. It's part of every child's education. They learn the principles of agriculture at school, and they're taken for regular outings into the fields near the town, where they not only watch farm-work being done, but also do some themselves, as a form of exercise.

Besides farming which, as I say, is everybody's job, each person is taught a special trade of his own. He may be trained to process wool or flax, or he may become a stonemason, a blacksmith, or a carpenter. Those are the only trades that employ any considerable quantity of labour. They have no tailors or dressmakers, since everyone on the island wears the same sort of clothes – except that they vary slightly according to sex and marital status – and the fashion never changes. These clothes are quite pleasant to look at, they allow free movement of the limbs, they're equally suitable for hot and cold weather – and the great thing is, they're all home-made. So everybody learns one of the other trades I mentioned, and by everybody I mean the women as well as the men – though the weaker sex are given the lighter job, like spinning and weaving, while the men do the heavier ones.

Most children are brought up to do the same work as their parents, since they tend to have a natural feeling for it. But if a child fancies some other trade, he's adopted into a family that practises it. Of course, great care is taken, not only by the father, but also by the local authorities, to see that the foster-father is a decent, respectable type. When you've learned one trade properly, you can, if you like, get permission to learn another – and when you're an expert in both, you can practise whichever you prefer, unless the other one is more essential to the public.

The chief business of the Stywards – in fact, practically their only business – is to see that nobody sits around doing nothing, but that everyone gets on with his job. They don't wear people out, though, by keeping them hard at work from early morning till late at night, like cart-horses. That's just slavery – and yet that's what life is like for the working classes nearly everywhere else in the world. In Utopia they have a six-hour working day – three hours in the morning, then lunch – then a two-hour break – then three more hours in the afternoon, followed by supper. They go to bed at 8 p.m., and sleep for eight hours. All the rest of the twenty-four they're free to do what they like – not to waste their time in idleness or self-indulgence, but to make good use of it in some congenial activity. Most people spend these free periods on further education, for there are public lectures first thing every morning. Attendance is quite voluntary, except for those picked out for academic training, but men and women of all classes go crowding in to hear them – I mean, different people go to different lectures, just as the spirit moves them. However, there's nothing to stop you from spending this extra time on your trade, if you want to. Lots of people do, if they haven't the capacity for intellectual work, and are much admired for such public-spirited behaviour.

After supper they have an hour's recreation, either in the gardens or in the communal dining-halls, according to the time of year. Some people practise music, others just talk. They've never heard of anything so silly and demoralizing as dice, but they have two games rather like chess. The first is a sort of arithmetical contest, in which certain numbers 'take' others. The second is a pitched battle between virtues and vices, which illustrates most ingeniously how vices tend to conflict with one another, but to combine against virtues. It also shows which vices are opposed to which virtues, how much strength vices can muster for a direct assault, what indirect tactics they employ, what help virtues need to overcome vices, what are the best methods of evading their attacks, and what ultimately determines the victory of one side or the other.

But here's a point that requires special attention, or you're liable to get the wrong idea. Since they only work a six-hour day, you may think there must be a shortage of essential goods. On the contrary, those six hours are enough, and more than enough to produce plenty of everything that's needed for a comfortable life. And you'll understand why it is, if you reckon up how large a proportion of the population in other countries is totally unemployed. First you have practically all the women – that gives you nearly fifty per cent for a start. And in countries where the women *do* work, the men tend to lounge about instead. Then there are all the priests, and members of so-called religious orders – how much work do they do? Add all the rich, especially the landowners, popularly known as nobles and gentlemen. Include their domestic staffs – I mean those gangs of armed ruffians that I mentioned before. Finally, throw in all the beggars who are perfectly hale and hearty, but pretend to be ill as an excuse for being lazy. When you've counted them up, you'll be surprised to find how few people actually produce what the human race consumes.

And now just think how few of these few people are doing essential work – for where money is the only standard of value, there are bound to be dozens of unnecessary trades carried on, which merely supply luxury goods or entertainment. Why, even if the existing labour force were distributed among the few trades really needed to make life reasonably comfortable, there'd be so much over-production that prices would fall too low for the workers to earn a living. Whereas, if you took all those engaged in non-essential trades, and all who are too lazy to work – each of whom consumes twice as much of the products of other people's labour as any of the producers themselves – if you put the whole lot of them on to something useful, you'd soon see how few hours' work a day would be amply sufficient to supply all the necessities and comforts of life – to which you might add all real and natural forms of pleasure.

But in Utopia the facts speak for themselves. There, out of all the able-bodied men and women who live in a town, or in the country round it, five hundred at the most are exempted from ordinary work. This includes the Stywards, who, though legally exempt, go on working voluntarily to set a good example. It also includes those who are permanently relieved of other duties so that they can concentrate on their studies. This privilege is only granted on the recommendation of the priests, confirmed by the Stywards in a secret ballot – and, if such a student produces disappointing results, he's sent back to the working class. On the other hand, it's not at all unusual for a manual worker to study so hard in his spare time, and make such good progress, that he's excused from practising his trade, and promoted to the intelligentsia.

This is the class from which the diplomats, priests, Bench-eaters, and of, course mayors are recruited. The old-fashioned word for a mayor, by the way, is *Barzanes*,[4] though nowadays he's usually called a Nopeople. As hardly any other member of the population is either unemployed or non-productively employed, you can guess how much good work they get done in a few hours. Their labour problem is also reduced by the fact that they tackle essential jobs with more economy of effort than we do. For instance, the reason why the building trade usually absorbs so much labour is that people put up houses which their improvident heirs allow to tumble down. So the next generation has to start building all over again, which costs infinitely more than it would have cost to keep the original houses standing. In fact, what often happens is this: A builds a very expensive house, which then fails to satisfy B's fastidious taste. B therefore neglects it so badly that it's soon in ruins, and builds himself an equally expensive house elsewhere. But in Utopia, where everything's under state control, houses are very seldom built on entirely new sites, and repairs are carried out immediately they become necessary, if not before. Thus they achieve maximum durability with the minimum of labour, which means that builders sometimes have practically nothing to do. On such occasions they're sent home to saw up planks and get stones ready squared, so that if they do have to build anything it can go up all the faster.

Then think how much labour they save on clothes. Their working clothes are just loose-fitting leather overalls, which last for at least seven years. When they go about in public, they cover these rough garments with a sort of cloak, which is always the same colour – the natural colour of wool. Thus not only is their consumption of woollen fabric the lowest in the world, but so are their production costs for this material. Linen is even easier to produce, and therefore more often used – but, as long as the linen is white and the wool is clean, they don't care how fine or coarse the thread is. So whereas in other countries you won't find anyone satisfied with less than five or six suits and as many silk shirts, while dressy types want over ten of each, your Utopian is content with a single piece of clothing every two years. For why should he want more? They wouldn't make him any warmer – or any better looking.

With everybody doing useful work, and with such work reduced to a minimum, they build up such large reserves of everything that from time to time they can release a huge labour force to mend any roads which are in bad condition. And quite often, if there's nothing of that sort to be done, the authorities announce a shorter working day. They never force people to work unnecessarily, for the main purpose of their whole economy is to give each person as much time free from physical drudgery as the needs of the community will allow, so that he can cultivate his mind – which they regard as the secret of a happy life.

Now I'd better explain their social arrangements – how society is organized, how they behave towards one another, how goods are distributed, and so on. Well, the smallest social unit is the household, which is virtually synonymous with the family. When a girl grows up and gets married, she joins her husband's household, but the boys of each generation stay at home, under the control of their oldest male relative – unless he becomes senile, in which case the next oldest takes over.

Each town consists of six thousand households, not counting the country ones, and to keep the population fairly steady there's a law that no household shall contain less than ten or more than sixteen adults – as they can't very well fix a figure for children. This law is observed by simply moving supernumerary adults to smaller households. If the town as a whole gets too full, the surplus population is transferred to a town that's comparatively empty. If the whole island becomes overpopulated, they tell off a certain number of people from each town to go and start a colony at the nearest point on the mainland where there's a large area that hasn't been cultivated by the local inhabitants. Such colonies are governed by the Utopians, but the natives are allowed to join in if they want to. When this happens, natives and colonists soon combine to form a single community with a single way of life, to the great advantage of both parties – for, under Utopian management, land which used to be thought incapable of producing anything for one lot of people produces plenty for two.

If the natives won't do what they're told, they're expelled from the area marked out for annexation. If they try to resist, the Utopians declare war – for they consider war perfectly justifiable, when one country denies another its natural right to derive nourishment from any soil which the original owners are not using themselves, but are merely holding on to as a worthless piece of property.

Should any town become so depopulated that it can't be brought up to strength by transfers from elsewhere on the island, without reducing the population of some other town below the prescribed minimum – a thing which is said to have happened only twice in their history, each time as the result of a violent epidemic – they recall colonists to fill the gap, on the principle that it's better to lose a colony than to weaken any part of Utopia itself.

But let's get back to their social organization. Each household, as I said, comes under the authority of the oldest male. Wives are subordinate to their husbands, children to their parents, and younger people generally to their elders. Every town is divided into four districts of equal size, each with its own shopping centre in the middle of it. There the products of every household are collected in warehouses, and then distributed according to type among various shops. When the head of a household needs anything for himself or his family, he just goes to one of these shops and asks for it. And whatever he asks for, he's allowed to take away without any sort of payment, either in money or in kind. After all, why shouldn't he? There's more than enough of everything to go round, so there's no risk of his asking for more than he needs – for why should anyone want to start hoarding, when he knows he'll never have to go short of anything? No living creature is naturally greedy, except from fear of want – or in the case of human beings, from vanity, the notion that you're better than people if you can display more superfluous property than they can. But there's no scope for that sort of thing in Utopia.

These shopping centres include provision markets, to which they take meat and fish, as well as bread, fruit and vegetables.

But there are special places outside the town where all blood and dirt are first washed off in running water. The slaughtering of livestock and cleaning of carcasses is done by slaves. They don't let ordinary people get used to cutting up animals, because they think it tends to destroy one's natural feelings of humanity. It's also forbidden to bring anything dirty or unhygienic inside the town, for fear of polluting the atmosphere and so causing disease.

Every so often, as you walk down a street, you come to a large building, which has a special name of its own. That's where the Styward lives, and where his thirty households – fifteen from one direction and fifteen from the other – have their meals. The caterers for such dining-halls go off at a certain time each day to the provision market, where they report the number of people registered with them, and draw the appropriate rations.

But hospital patients get first priority – oh yes, there are four hospitals in the suburbs, just outside the walls. Each of them is about the size of a small town. The idea of this is to prevent overcrowding, and facilitate the isolation of infectious cases. These hospitals are so well run, and so well supplied with all types of medical equipment, the nurses are so sympathetic and conscientious, and there are so many experienced doctors constantly available, that, though nobody's forced to go there, practically everyone would rather be ill in hospitals than at home.

However, once the caterers for the hospital have got what the doctors have ordered, all the best food that's left is divided equally among the dining-halls – that is, in proportion to the number registered at each – except that certain people receive preferential treatment, such as the Mayor, the Bishop, Bench-eaters, and diplomats. The same applies to foreigners – not that there often are any; but, when there are, they're provided with special furnished accommodation.

At lunch-time and supper-time a bugle is blown, and the whole Sty assembles in the dining-hall – except for anyone who's in hospital or ill at home. However, you're quite at liberty to take food home from the market, once the dining-halls have been supplied, for everyone knows you wouldn't do it unless you had to. I mean, no one likes eating at home, although there's no rule against it. For one thing, it's considered rather

bad form. For another, it seems silly to go to all the trouble
of preparing an inferior meal, when there's an absolutely
delicious one waiting for you at the dining-hall just down the
street.

In these dining-halls all the rough and dirty work is done by
slaves, but the actual business of preparing and cooking the
food, and planning the menus, is left entirely to the women of
the household on duty – for a different household is responsible
for providing the meals every day. The rest of the adults sit
at three tables or more, according to their numbers, with the
men against the wall and the women on the outside – so that if
they suddenly feel sick, as pregnant women do from time to
time, they can get up without disturbing anyone else, and retire
to the nursery.

By the nursery I mean a room reserved for nursing mothers
and their babies, where there's always a good fire and plenty of
clean water. There are also plenty of cots, so that mothers can
either put their babies to bed, or, if they like, undress them and
let them play in front of the fire. Babies are always breast-fed by
their mothers, except when death or illness makes this impossible, in which case the Styward's wife takes immediate
steps to find a wet-nurse. This presents no problem, for any
woman who's in a position to do so will be only too glad to
volunteer for the job. You see, such acts of mercy are universally
admired, and the child itself will always regard her as its real
mother.

The nursery is also the place where the under-fives have their
meals. The other children, that is, all boys and girls who aren't
old enough to be married, wait at table in the dining-room, or if
they're too young for that, just stand there and keep absolutely
quiet. In neither case do they have a separate meal-time – they're
fed from the tables of the grown-ups.

The place of honour is the centre of the high table, which is
on a platform across the end of the hall, and so commands a
view of the whole company. Here sit the Styward and his wife,
with two of the oldest residents – for the seating is always
arranged in groups of four. If there happens to be a church
in the Sty, the priest and his wife automatically take precedence,
and sit with the Styward. On either side of them are four younger

people, then four more older ones, and so on right round the
hall. In other words, you sit with your contemporaries, but
you're also made to mix with a different age group. The theory
of this, I'm told, is that respect for the older generation tends
to discourage bad behaviour among the younger ones – since
everything they say or do is bound to be noticed by the people
sitting just beside them.

Whey they're handing out food, they don't work straight
along the table from one end to the other. They start by giving
the best helpings to the older groups, whose places are clearly
marked, and then serve equal portions to the others. However,
if there's not enough of some particular delicacy to go round,
the older ones share their helpings, as they think fit, with their
neighbours. Thus the privilege of age is duly respected – but
everyone gets just as much in the end.

Lunch and supper begin with a piece of improving literature
read aloud – but they keep it quite short, so that nobody gets
bored. Then the older people start discussing serious problems,
but not in a humourless or depressing way. Nor do they monopolize the conversation throughout the meal. On the contrary,
they enjoy listening to the young ones, and deliberately draw
them out, so that they can gauge each person's character and
intelligence, as they betray themselves in a relaxed, informal
atmosphere.

Lunch is pretty short, because work comes after it, but over
supper they rather spread themselves, since it's followed by a
whole night's sleep, which they consider more conducive to
sound digestion. During supper they always have music, and
the meal ends with a great variety of sweets and fruit. They also
burn incense, and spray the hall with scent. In fact, they do
everything they can to make people enjoy themselves – for
they're rather inclined to believe that all harmless pleasures
are perfectly legitimate.

Well, that's what life is like in the towns. In the country,
because of the greater distances involved, everyone eats at
home. Of course, they have just as good food as they'd have
in town – for they're the ones who produce what the town-
dwellers eat.

Now about travel facilities. If you want to visit friends in some other town, or would simply like to see the town itself, you can easily get permission to go there, unless you're urgently needed at home, by applying to your Styward and your Bench-eater. You'll be sent with a party of people travelling on a group passport, signed by the Mayor, which says when you've got to be back. You'll be offered some sort of vehicle, with a slave to drive the oxen and look after them – but, unless there are women in the party, most people find this more trouble than it's worth, and prefer to do without. You needn't take any luggage, for wherever you go you'll be equally at home, and able to get everything you want. If you stay in any place for more than twenty-four hours, you'll be expected to carry on with your ordinary work – and be welcomed with open arms by the other people who do it there.

If you're caught without a passport outside your own district, you're brought home in disgrace, and severely punished as a deserter. For a second offence the punishment is slavery. How-ever, if you feel the urge to go wandering about the countryside near the town, there's nothing to stop your doing so, provided your father gives his permission, and your wife doesn't object. Of course, you won't be able to get a meal anywhere, until you've done either a morning's or an afternoon's work there – but, apart from that, you're free to go wherever you like within the territory of your own town, and you're just as useful a member of society as if you'd stayed at home.

You see how it is – wherever you are, you always have to work. There's never any excuse for idleness. There are also no wine-taverns, no ale-houses, no brothels, no opportunities for seduction, no secret meeting-places. Everyone has his eye on you, so you're practically forced to get on with your job, and make some proper use of your spare time.

Under such a system, there's bound to be plenty of every-thing, and, as everything is divided equally among the entire population, there obviously can't be any poor people or beggars. Each town, you remember, sends three representatives to the annual Lietalk, or Parliament, at Aircastle. There they collect details of the year's production, and as soon as it's clear which products are plentiful in each area, and which are in short supply, they arrange for a series of transfers to equalize distribution. These transfers are one-way transactions, requiring nothing in return – but in practice the free gifts that Town A makes to Town B are balanced by the free gifts that it receives from Town C. So the whole island is like one big household.

When they've made adequate provision for their own needs – which they don't consider they've done, until their reserves are big enough to last them for a year, no matter what happens during the next twelve months – the remainder is exported. Such exports include vast quantities of corn, honey, wool, flax, timber, scarlet and purple cloth, rawhide, wax, tallow, leather, and livestock. One seventh of their total exports to any country go as a free gift to the poor – the rest they sell at reasonable prices. This foreign trade not only pays for essential imports – which normally means just iron – but also brings in a great deal of money. In fact, over a long period they've built up incredibly large reserves of gold and silver. So nowadays they don't much care whether they sell for cash or on credit, and nearly all their trade is of the second kind. However, when giving credit, they're not content with private securities, but insist on having a legal contract signed, sealed, and delivered by the local authority of the importing area. When payment becomes due, this authority collects the money from the individuals concerned, puts it in the public funds, and enjoys the use of it until such time as the Utopians call it in – which they practically never do, for they think it unfair to deprive other people of anything that's useful to them, if one doesn't need it oneself.

However, if they find it necessary to lend part of this capital to another country, then they do ask for it back – and so they do in wartime, for war is the one thing they have in mind when accumulating all that wealth. You see, it's meant to protect them in the event of any major crisis or emergency. Its chief function is to provide colossal rates of pay for foreign mercenaries – whose lives they risk more willingly than their own. They're also well aware that even enemies can be bribed, if you offer them enough, to betray one another or start fighting among themselves. And that's the only reason why they keep such huge stocks of precious metals. Not that *they* regard them as precious. In fact, I hardly like to tell you how they do regard them, for fear you shouldn't believe me – a fear which seems all the more reasonable when I think how difficult I'd have found it to believe myself, if I hadn't seen it with my own eyes. For things always sound incredible if they're remote from one's own habits of thought. Still, I suppose it's rather illogical to be surprised at the way they use silver and gold, considering how different all their other customs are from ours. I'm thinking particularly of the fact that they don't use money themselves, but merely keep it for use in an emergency which may or may not arise.

In the meantime silver and gold, the raw materials of money, get no more respect from anyone than their intrinsic value deserves – which is obviously far less than that of iron. Without iron human life is simply impossible, just as it is without fire or water – but we could easily do without silver and gold, if it weren't for the idiotic concept of scarcity-value.[5] And yet kind Mother Nature has deliberately placed all her greatest blessings, like earth, air, and water, right under our noses, and tucked away out of sight the things that are no use to us.

Now if they locked these metals up in a strong-room, the man in the street might get some silly idea into his head – you know what a talent he has for that kind of thing – that the Mayor and the Bencheaters were cheating him, and somehow making a profit out of the stuff. It could, of course, be converted into ornamental bowls or other *objets d'art*. But then people would grow so fond of them that, if they ever had to melt them down and pay soldiers with them, it would be a terrible wrench.

To get around these difficulties, they've devised a system which, while perfectly consistent with their other conventions, is diametrically opposed to ours – especially to the way we treasure up gold. So you'll probably think it incredible, until you've actually seen it for yourselves. According to this system, plates and drinking-vessels, though beautifully designed, are made of quite cheap stuff like glass or earthenware. But silver and gold are the normal materials, in private houses as well as communal dining-halls, for the humblest items of domestic equipment, such as chamber-pots. They also use chains and fetters of solid gold to immobilize slaves, and anyone who commits a really shameful crime is forced to go about with gold rings on his ears and fingers, a gold necklace round his neck, and a crown of gold on his head. In fact they do everything they can to bring these metals into contempt. This means that if they suddenly had to part with all the gold and silver they possess – a fate which in any other country would be thought equivalent to having one's guts torn out – nobody in Utopia would care two hoots.

It's much the same with jewels. There are pearls to be found on the beaches, diamonds and garnets on certain types of rock – but they never bother to look for them. However, if they happen to come across one, they pick it up and polish it for some toddler to wear. At first, children are terribly proud of such jewellery – until they're old enough to register that it's only worn in the nursery. Then, without any prompting from their parents, but purely as a matter of self-respect, they give it up – just as our children grow out of things like dolls, and conkers, and lucky charms. This curious convention is liable to cause some equally curious reactions, as I realized most vividly in the case of the Flatulentine diplomats.

These diplomats visited Aircastle while I was there, and, as they were coming to discuss a matter of great importance, each town had sent its three members of parliament to meet them. Now all foreign diplomats who'd been there before had come from places just across the channel, and were therefore quite familiar with Utopian ideas. They knew it was a country where expensive clothes were not admired, silk was despised, and gold was a dirty word, so they'd dressed as simply as they could for the occasion. But these Flatulentines lived too far away to have had much contact with the Utopians. All they knew was that everyone in Utopia wore the same sort of clothes, and pretty crude ones at that – presumably because they'd nothing better to wear. So they adopted a policy more arrogant than diplomatic, which was to array themselves in positively godlike splendour, and dazzle the wretched Utopians with their magnificence.

When the legation arrived, it consisted of only three men, but these were escorted by a hundred retainers, all wearing multi-coloured clothes, mostly made of silk. As for the great men themselves – for they *were* great men in their own country –

they wore cloth of gold, with great gold chains round their necks, gold ear-rings dangling from their ears, and gold rings on their fingers. Their very hats were festooned with glittering ropes of pearls and other jewels. In fact they were fully equipped with all the things used in Utopia for punishing slaves, humiliating criminals, or amusing small children.

Well, I wouldn't have missed it for anything. There were these three gentlemen, looking terribly pleased with themselves, as they compared their own appearance with that of the local inhabitants – for of course the streets were packed with people. And there was the actual effect that they were producing – so very unexpected and disappointing. You see, from the Utopians' point of view – apart from a few who'd had occasion to go abroad – all that splendour was merely degrading. So they reserved their most respectful greeting for the least distinguished members of the party, and completely ignored the diplomats themselves, assuming from their gold chains that they must be slaves.

Oh, but you should have seen the faces of the older children, who'd grown out of things like pearls and jewels, when they saw the ones on the envoys' hats. They kept nudging their mothers and whispering:

'I say, Mother, just look at that great baby! Fancy wearing jewellery at his age!'

To which the mother would reply, very seriously:

'Sh, dear! I imagine he must be a clown attached to the embassy.'

The gold chains also came in for a lot of criticism.

'I don't think much of that chain,' someone would say. 'It's so thin, the slave could easily break it. Besides, it's far too loose. He could wriggle out of it any time he liked, and run off scot-free!'

But when they'd been there for a day or two, the Flatulentines began to realize the situation. They saw that gold was plentiful, and held extremely cheap – in fact despised as heartily as they themselves admired it. They also noticed that a single runaway slave carried more silver and gold on his person than the three of them put together. So eventually they stopped trying to show off, and, feeling rather ashamed of themselves, abandoned all the finery that they'd been so proud of – especially after a few friendly talks with their hosts, which gave them some insight into local conventions and attitudes. For instance, the Utopians fail to understand why anyone should be so fascinated by the dull gleam of a tiny bit of stone, when he has all the stars in the sky to look at – or how anyone can be silly enough to think himself better than other people, because his clothes are made of finer woollen thread than theirs. After all, those fine clothes were once worn by a sheep, and they never turned it into anything better than a sheep.[6]

Nor can they understand why a totally useless substance like gold should now, all over the world, be considered far more important than human beings, who gave it such value as it has, purely for their own convenience. The result is that a man with about as much mental agility as a lump of lead or a block of wood, a man whose utter stupidity is paralleled only by his immorality, can have lots of good, intelligent people at his beck and call, just because he happens to possess a large pile of gold coins. And if by some freak of fortune or trick of the law – two equally effective methods of turning things upside down – the said coins were suddenly transferred to the most worthless member of his domestic staff, you'd soon see the present owner trotting after his money, like an extra piece of currency, and becoming his own servant's servant. But what puzzles and disgusts the Utopians even more is the idiotic way some people have of practically worshipping a rich man, not because they owe him money or are otherwise in his power, but simply because he's rich – although they know perfectly well that he's far too mean to let a single penny come their way, so long as he's alive to stop it.

They get these ideas partly from being brought up under a social system which is directly opposed to that type of nonsense, and partly from their reading and education. Admittedly, no one's allowed to become a full-time student, except for the very few in each town who appear as children to possess unusual gifts, outstanding intelligence, and a special aptitude for academic research. But every child receives a primary education, and most men and women go on educating themselves all their lives during those free periods that I told you about. Everything's taught in their own language, for it has quite a rich vocabulary. It's also quite pleasant to listen to, and extremely expressive. People are beginning to speak it all over that part of the world – though always in a more or less debased form.

Until we arrived, they didn't even know the name of any famous European philosopher. And yet they'd discovered much the same principles, in music, logic, arithmetic, and geometry, as those early authorities of ours. But though in most things they're on a par with the Ancients, they're no match for the Moderns when it comes to logic. For instance, they've still failed to invent a single one of those rules about Restrictions, Amplifications, and Suppositions which have been so cleverly worked out in *A Short Introduction to Logic*,[7] for all our school-boys to learn by heart. And so far from being equal to investigating Second Intentions,[8] they're even blind to the existence of that notorious Universal, M A N.[9] Now he, as you know, is a pretty conspicuous figure, bigger than any giant you ever heard of – but, though we pointed him out quite clearly, none of them could see him.

On the other hand they're great experts in astronomy,[10] and have invented several ingenious instruments for determining the precise positions and movements of the sun and moon, and of all other heavenly bodies visible in their hemisphere. But as for astrology – friendships and quarrels between the planets, fortune-telling by the stars, and all the rest of that humbug – they've never even dreamt of such a thing.

They've learnt by long experience to recognize the signs of approaching rain, wind, and other changes in the weather. But if you asked them to explain the theory of such phenomena, or to say why the sea is salt, or what causes tides, or to give a general account of the origin and nature of the universe, you'd get various different answers. Some of them would be in line with the views of our ancient philosophers. However, as these weren't always unanimous, you won't be surprised to hear that the Utopians have produced some entirely new theories of their own, which aren't wholly consistent with one another either.

In ethics they discuss the same problems as we do. Having distinguished between three types of 'good', psychological, physiological, and environmental, they proceed to ask whether the term is strictly applicable to all of them, or only to the first. They also argue about such things as virtue and pleasure. But their chief subject of dispute is the nature of human happiness – on what factor or factors does it depend? Here they seem rather too much inclined to take a hedonistic view, for according to them human happiness consists largely or wholly in pleasure. Surprisingly enough, they defend this self-indulgent doctrine by arguments drawn from religion – a thing normally associated with a more serious view of life, if not with gloomy asceticism. You see, in all their discussions of happiness they invoke certain religious principles to supplement the operations of reason, which they think otherwise ill-equipped to identify true happiness.

The first principle is that every soul is immortal, and was created by a kind God, Who meant it to be happy. The second is that we shall be rewarded or punished in the next world for our good or bad behaviour in this one. Although these are religious principles, the Utopians find rational grounds for accepting them. For suppose you didn't accept them? In that case, they say, any fool could tell you what you ought to do. You should go all out for your own pleasure, irrespective of right and wrong. You'd merely have to make sure that minor pleasures didn't interfere with major ones, and avoid the type of pleasure that has painful after-effects. For what's the sense of struggling to be virtuous, denying yourself the pleasant things of life, and deliberately making yourself uncomfortable, if there's nothing you hope to gain by it? And what *can* you hope to gain by it, if you receive no compensation after death for a thoroughly unpleasant, that is, a thoroughly miserable life?

Not that they identify happiness with every type of pleasure – only with the higher ones. Nor do they identify it with virtue – unless they belong to a quite different school of thought. According to the normal view, happiness is the *summum bonum* towards which we're naturally impelled by virtue – which in their definition means following one's natural impulses,[11] as God meant us to do. But this includes obeying the instinct to be reasonable in our likes and dislikes. And reason also teaches us, first to love and reverence Almighty God, to Whom we owe our existence and our potentiality for happiness, and secondly to get through life as comfortably and cheerfully as we can, and help all other members of our species to do so too.

The fact is, even the sternest ascetic tends to be slightly inconsistent in his condemnation of pleasure. He may sentence *you* to a life of hard labour, inadequate sleep, and general discomfort, but he'll also tell you to do your best to ease the pains and privations of others. He'll regard all such attempts to improve the human situation as laudable acts of humanity – for obviously nothing could be more humane, or more natural for a human being, than to relieve other people's sufferings, put an end to their miseries, and restore their *joie de vivre,* that is, their capacity for pleasure. So why shouldn't it be equally natural to do the same thing for oneself?

Either it's a bad thing to enjoy life, in other words, to experience pleasure – in which case you shouldn't help anyone to do it, but should try to save the whole human race from such a frightful fate – or else, if it's good for other people, and you're not only allowed, but positively obliged to make it possible for them, why shouldn't charity begin at home? After all, you've a duty to yourself as well as to your neighbour, and, if Nature says you must be kind to others, she can't turn round the next moment and say you must be cruel to yourself. The Utopians therefore regard the enjoyment of life – that is, pleasure – as the natural object of all human efforts, and natural, as they define it, is synonymous with virtuous. However, Nature also wants us to help one another to enjoy life, for the very good reason that no human being has a monopoly of her affections. She's equally anxious for the welfare of every member of the species. So of course she tells us to make quite sure that we don't pursue our own interests at the expense of other people's.

On this principle they think it right to keep one's promises in private life, and also to obey public laws for regulating the distribution of 'goods' – by which I mean the raw materials of pleasure – provided such laws have been properly made by a wise ruler, or passed by common consent of a whole population, which has not been subjected to any form of violence or deception. Within these limits they say it's sensible to consult one's own interests, and a moral duty to consult those of the community as well. It's wrong to deprive someone else of a pleasure so that you can enjoy one yourself, but to deprive yourself of a pleasure so that you can add to someone else's enjoyment is an act of humanity by which you always gain more than you lose. For one thing, such benefits are usually repaid in kind. For another, the mere sense of having done somebody a kindness, and so earned his affection and good will, produces a spiritual satisfaction which far outweighs the loss of a physical one. And lastly – a belief that comes easily to a religious mind – God will reward us for such small sacrifices of momentary pleasure, by giving us an eternity of perfect joy. Thus they argue that, in the final analysis, pleasure is the ultimate happiness which all human beings have in view, even when they're acting most virtuously.

Pleasure they define as any state or activity, physical or mental, which is naturally enjoyable. The operative word is *naturally*. According to them, we're impelled by reason as well as an instinct to enjoy ourselves in any natural way which doesn't hurt other people, interfere with greater pleasures, or cause unpleasant after-effects. But human beings have entered into an idiotic conspiracy to call some things enjoyable which are naturally nothing of the kind – as though facts were as easily changed as definitions. Now the Utopians believe that, so far from contributing to happiness, this type of thing makes happiness impossible – because, once you get used to it, you lose all capacity for real pleasure, and are merely obsessed by illusory forms of it. Very often these have nothing pleasant about them at all – in fact, most of them are thoroughly disagreeable. But they appeal so strongly to perverted tastes that they come to be reckoned not only among the major pleasures of life, but even among the chief reasons for living.

In the category of illusory pleasure-addicts they include the kind of person I mentioned before, who thinks himself better than other people because he's better dressed than they are. Actually he's just as wrong about his clothes as he is about himself. From a practical point of view, why is it better to be dressed in fine woollen thread than in coarse? But he's got it into his head that fine thread is naturally superior, and that wearing it somehow increases his own value. So he feels entitled to far more respect than he'd ever dare to hope for, if he were less expensively dressed, and is most indignant if he fails to get it.

Talking of respect, isn't it equally idiotic to attach such importance to a lot of empty gestures which do nobody any good? For what real pleasure can you get out of the sight of a bared head or a bent knee? Will it cure the rheumatism in your own knee, or make you any less weak in the head? Of course, the great believers in this type of artificial pleasure are those who pride themselves on their 'nobility'. Nowadays that merely means that they happen to belong to a family which has been rich for several generations, preferably in landed property. And yet they feel every bit as 'noble' even if they've failed to inherit any of the said property, or if they have inherited it and then frittered it all away.

Then there's another type of person I mentioned before, who has a passion for jewels, and feels practically superhuman if he manages to get hold of a rare one, especially if it's a kind that's considered particularly precious in his country and period – for the value of such things varies according to where and when you live. But he's so terrified of being taken in by appearances that he refuses to buy any jewel until he's stripped off all the gold and inspected it in the nude. And even then he won't buy it without a solemn assurance and a written guarantee from the jeweller that the stone is genuine. But my dear sir, why shouldn't a fake give you just as much pleasure, if you can't, with your own eyes, distinguish it from a real one? It makes no difference to you whether it's genuine or not – any more than it would to a blind man!

And now, what about those people who accumulate superfluous wealth, for no better purpose than to enjoy looking at it? Is their pleasure a real one, or merely a form of delusion? The opposite type of psychopath buries his gold, so that he'll never be able to use it, and may never even see it again. In fact, he deliberately loses it in his anxiety not to lose it – for what can you call it but lost, when it's put back into the earth, where it's no good to him, or probably to anyone else? And yet he's tremendously happy when he's got it stowed away. Now, apparently, he can stop worrying. But suppose the money is stolen, and ten years later he dies without ever knowing it has gone. Then for a whole ten years he has managed to survive his loss, and during that period what difference has it made to him whether the money was there or not? It was just as little use to him either way.[12]

Among stupid pleasures they include not only gambling – a form of idiocy that they've heard about but never practised – but also hunting and hawking. What on earth is the fun, they ask, of throwing dice on to a table? Besides, you've done it so often that, even if there was some fun in it at first, you must surely be sick of it by now. How can you possibly enjoy listening to anything so disagreeable as the barking and howling of dogs? And why is it more amusing to watch a dog chasing a hare than to watch one dog chasing another? In each case the essential activity is running – if running is what amuses you. But if it's really the thought of being in at the death, and seeing an animal torn to pieces before your eyes, wouldn't pity be a more appropriate reaction to the sight of a weak, timid, harmless little creature like a hare being devoured by something so much stronger and fiercer?

So the Utopians consider hunting below the dignity of free men, and leave it entirely to butchers, who are, as I told you, slaves. In their view hunting is the vilest department of butchery, compared with which all the others are relatively useful and honourable. An ordinary butcher slaughters livestock far more sparingly,[13] and only because he has to, whereas a hunter kills and mutilates poor little creatures purely for his own amusement. They say you won't find that type of blood-lust even among animals, unless they're particularly savage by nature, or have become so by constantly being used for this cruel sport.

There are hundreds of things like that, which are generally regarded as pleasures, but everyone in Utopia is quite convinced that they've got nothing to do with real pleasure, because there's nothing naturally enjoyable about them. Nor is this conviction at all shaken by the argument that most people do actually enjoy them, which would seem to indicate an appreciable pleasure-content. They say this is a purely subjective reaction caused by bad habits, which can make a person prefer unpleasant things to pleasant ones, just as pregnant women sometimes lose their sense of taste, and find suet or turpentine more delicious than honey. But however much one's judgement may be impaired by habit or ill health, the nature of pleasure, as of everything else, remains unchanged.

Real pleasures they divide into two categories, mental and physical. Mental pleasures include the satisfaction that one gets from understanding something, or from contemplating truth. They also include the memory of a well-spent life, and the confident expectation of good things to come. Physical pleasures are subdivided into two types. First there are those which fill the whole organism with a conscious sense of enjoyment. This may be the result of replacing physical substances which have been burnt up by the natural heat of the body, as when we eat or drink. Or else it may be caused by the discharge of some excess, as in excretion, sexual intercourse, or any relief of irritation by rubbing or scratching. However, there are also pleasures which satisfy no organic need, and relieve no previous discomfort. They merely act, in a mysterious but quite unmistakable way, directly on our senses, and monopolize their reactions. Such is the pleasure of music.

Their second type of physical pleasure arises from the calm and regular functioning of the body – that is, from a state of health undisturbed by any minor ailments. In the absence of mental discomfort, this gives one a good feeling, even without the help of external pleasures. Of course, it's less ostentatious, and forces itself less violently on one's attention than the cruder delights of eating and drinking, but even so it's often considered the greatest pleasure in life. Practically everyone in Utopia would agree that it's a very important one, because it's the basis of all the others. It's enough by itself to make you enjoy life, and unless you have it, no other pleasure is possible. However, mere freedom from pain, without positive health, they would call not pleasure but anaesthesia.

Some thinkers used to maintain that a uniformly tranquil state of health couldn't properly be termed a pleasure since its presence could only be detected by contrast with its opposite – oh yes, they went very thoroughly into the whole question. But that theory was exploded long ago, and nowadays nearly everybody subscribes to the view that health is most definitely a pleasure. The argument goes like this – illness involves pain, which is the direct opposite of pleasure, and illness is the direct opposite of health, therefore health involves pleasure. They don't think it matters whether you say that illness *is* or merely *involves* pain. Either way it comes to the same thing. Similarly, whether health *is* a pleasure, or merely *produces* pleasure as inevitably as fire produces heat, it's equally logical to assume that where you have an uninterrupted state of health you cannot fail to have pleasure.

Besides, they say, when we eat something, what really happens is this. Our failing health starts fighting off the attacks of hunger,[14] using the food as an ally. Gradually it begins to prevail, and, in this very process of winning back its normal strength, experiences the sense of enjoyment which we find so refreshing. Now, if health enjoys the actual battle, why shouldn't it also enjoy the victory? Or are we to suppose that when it has finally managed to regain its former vigour – the one thing that it has been fighting for all this time – it promptly falls into a coma, and fails to notice or take advantage of its success? As for the idea that one isn't conscious of health except through its opposite, they say that's quite untrue. Everyone's perfectly aware of feeling well, unless he's asleep or actually feeling ill. Even the most insensitive and apathetic sort of person will admit that it's delightful to be healthy – and what is delight, but a synonym for pleasure?

They're particularly fond of mental pleasures, which they consider of primary importance, and attribute mostly to good behaviour and a clear conscience. Their favourite physical pleasure is health. Of course, they believe in enjoying food, drink, and so forth, but purely in the interests of health, for they don't regard such things as very pleasant in themselves – only as methods of resisting the stealthy onset of disease. A sensible person, they say, prefers keeping well to taking medicine, and would rather feel cheerful than have people trying to comfort him. On the same principle it's better not to need this type of pleasure than to become addicted to it. For, if you think that sort of thing will make you happy, you'll have to admit that your idea of perfect felicity would be a life consisting entirely of hunger, thirst, itching, eating, drinking, rubbing, and scratching[15] – which would obviously be most unpleasant as well as quite disgusting. Undoubtedly these pleasures should come right at the bottom of the list, because they're so impure. For instance, the pleasure of eating is invariably diluted with the pain of hunger, and not in equal proportions either – for the pain is both more intense and more prolonged. It starts before the pleasure, and doesn't stop until the pleasure has stopped too.

So they don't think much of pleasures like that, except in so far as they're necessary. But they enjoy them all the same, and feel most grateful to Mother Nature for encouraging her children to do things that have to be done so often, by making them so attractive. For just think how dreary life would be, if those chronic ailments, hunger and thirst, could only be cured by foul-tasting medicines, like the rarer types of disease!

They attach great value to special natural gifts such as beauty, strength, and agility. They're also keen on the pleasures of sight, hearing, and smell, which are peculiar to human beings – for no other species admires the beauty of the world, enjoys any sort of scent, except as a method of locating food, or can tell the difference between a harmony and a discord. They say these things give a sort of relish to life.

However, in all such matters they observe the rule that minor pleasures mustn't interfere with major ones, and that pleasure mustn't cause pain – which they think is bound to happen, if the pleasure is immoral. But they'd never dream of despising their own beauty, overtaxing their strength, converting their agility into inertia, ruining their physique by going without food, damaging their health, or spurning any other of Nature's gifts, unless they were doing it for the benefit of other people or of society, in the hope of receiving some greater pleasure from God in return. For they think it's quite absurd to torment oneself in the name of an unreal virtue, which does nobody any good, or in order to steel oneself against disasters which may never occur. They say such behaviour is merely self-destructive, and shows a most ungrateful attitude towards Nature – as if one refused all her favours, because one couldn't bear the thought of being indebted to her for anything.

Well, that's their ethical theory, and short of some divine

revelation, they doubt if the human mind is capable of devising a better one. We've no time to discuss whether it's right or wrong – nor is it really necessary, for all I undertook was to describe their way of life, not to defend it.

But one thing I'm quite sure of. Whatever you may think of their doctrines, you won't find a more prosperous country or a more splendid lot of people anywhere on earth. Physically, they're very active, full of energy, and stronger than their height would suggest – though you couldn't call them exactly short. Their land isn't always very fertile, and their climate's not too good, but by a well-balanced diet they build up their resistance to bad weather conditions, and by careful cultivation they correct the deficiencies of the soil. The result is that they've beaten all records for the production of corn and livestock, their expectation of life is the highest in the world, and their disease-rate the lowest. Thus, by scientific methods, they've done wonders with a country that's naturally rather barren. Not that their talents are confined to ordinary farming. You'll also find them uprooting whole forests and replanting them elsewhere, not to increase the yield, but to facilitate the transport of timber, by bringing it nearer to the sea, or to a river, or to a town – for it's not so easy to carry timber long distances by roads as corn. The people themselves are friendly and intelligent, with a good sense of humour. Though fond of relaxation, they're capable of hard physical work when necessary. Otherwise they don't much care for it – but they never get tired of using their brains.

When I told them about Greek literature and philosophy – for I didn't think there was anything in Latin that they'd like very much – they became extraordinarily anxious to study the original texts, under my tuition. So I started giving them lessons, at first merely because I didn't like to refuse, rather than from any hope of getting good results. But I soon realized that with such hard-working pupils my own efforts wouldn't be wasted. They had so little difficulty with the letters and pronunciation, learned things so quickly by heart and repeated them so accurately, that I'd have thought it quite miraculous, if I hadn't known that everyone who'd volunteered for the course, and got permission from the Council to join it, was a mature scholar of

outstanding intelligence. So in less than three years they knew
the language perfectly, and, apart from corruptions in the text,
there was nothing to stop them from reading straight through
any good author.

My own guess is that Greek somehow came naturally to
them, and that's why they found it so easy to learn. You see, I
can't help thinking they must be of Greek extraction, since
their language, though otherwise more like Persian, contains
some traces of Greek[16] in place-names and official titles. I presented them with several Greek texts – for when I started out
on the fourth voyage I didn't intend to come back for a very
long time, if at all, so, instead of packing a lot of things to sell,
I took on board a pretty large trunk full of books. I gave them
most of Plato, even more of Aristotle, and Theophrastus's work
on botany – but this, I'm sorry to say, was in rather poor condition, as I'd carelessly left it lying around while we were at sea,
and a monkey[17] had got hold of it. He'd amused himself by
playfully ripping out odd pages here and there, and tearing
them to pieces. The only grammar I could let them have was the
one by Lascaris,[18] for I hadn't brought my Theodorus[19] with
me, and their only dictionaries are those of Hesychius[20] and
Dioscorides.[21] They've also got Plutarch, who is their favourite
author, and Lucian, whom they find delightfully entertaining.
The poets are represented by Aristophanes, Homer, and Euri-
pides – oh yes, and Sophocles – in the miniature Aldine edition,
and the historians by Thucydides and Herodotus, not to mention Herodianus.[22]

My friend Tommy Rot had also brought some medical text-
books with him, a few short works by Hippocrates, and Galen's
Handbook.[23] The Utopians think very highly of them, for,
though nobody in the world needs medicine less than they do,
nobody has more respect for it. They consider it one of the most
interesting and important departments of science – and, as they
see it, the scientific investigation of nature is not only a most
enjoyable process, but also the best possible method of pleasing
the Creator. For they assume that He has the normal reactions
of an artist. Having put the marvellous system of the universe
on show for human beings to look at – since no other species is
capable of taking it in – He must prefer the type of person who

examines it carefully, and really admires His work, to the type
that just ignores it and like the lower animals remains quite
unimpressed by the whole astonishing spectacle.

By applying their trained intelligence to scientific research,
they've become amazingly good at inventing things that are
useful in everyday life. Two inventions, however, they owe
to us – though even there much of the credit should go to
them. For the moment we showed them some books that Aldus[24]
had printed, and talked a bit about printing and paper-making –
we couldn't explain them properly, as none of us knew much
about either process – they immediately made a shrewd guess
how the things were done. Up till then they'd only produced
skin, bark, or papyrus manuscripts, but now they instantly
started to manufacture paper, and print from type. At first they
weren't too successful, but after repeated experiments they
soon mastered both techniques so thoroughly that, if it weren't
for the shortage of original texts, they could have all the Greek
books they wanted. As it is, they have only the works I mentioned, but of these they've already printed and published
several thousand copies.

They welcome foreign tourists with open arms, if they've any
special talents to recommend them, or have done a lot of
travelling and know about many different countries. That's
why they were so glad to see us, for they love hearing what goes
on in other parts of the world. But traders don't often call there,
for apart from gold and silver, which most traders would rather
take home with them, the Utopians import nothing but iron.
As for their own export trade, they prefer to deliver things
themselves than have people come and fetch them, as this gives
them more experience of the outside world, and more practice
in navigation.

By the way, the slaves that I've occasionally referred to are
not, as you might imagine, non-combatant prisoners-of-war,[25]
slaves by birth, or purchases from foreign slave markets.
They're either Utopian convicts or, much more often, condemned criminals from other countries, who are acquired in
large numbers, sometimes for a small payment, but usually for
nothing. Both types of slaves are kept hard at work in chain-
gangs, though Utopians are treated worse than foreigners. The

idea is that it's all the more deplorable if a person who has had the advantage of a first-rate education and a thoroughly moral upbringing still insists on becoming a criminal – so the punishment should be all the more severe.

Another type of slave is the working-class foreigner who, rather than live in wretched poverty at home, volunteers for slavery in Utopia. Such people are treated with respect, and with almost as much kindness as Utopian citizens, except that they're made to work harder, because they're used to it. If they want to leave the country, which doesn't often happen, they're perfectly free to do so, and receive a small gratuity.

As I told you, when people are ill, they're looked after most sympathetically, and given everything in the way of medicine or special food that could possibly assist their recovery. In the case of permanent invalids, the nurses try to make them feel better by sitting and talking to them, and do all they can to relieve their symptoms. But if, besides being incurable, the disease also causes constant excruciating pain, some priests and government officials visit the person concerned, and say something like this:

'Let's face it, you'll never be able to live a normal life. You're just a nuisance to other people and a burden to yourself – in fact you're really leading a sort of posthumous existence. So why go on feeding germs? Since your life's a misery to you, why hesitate to die? You're imprisoned in a torture-chamber – why don't you break out and escape to a better world? Or say the word, and we'll arrange for your release. It's only common sense to cut your losses. It's also an act of piety to take the advice of a priest, because he speaks for God.'

If the patient finds these arguments convincing, he either starves himself to death, or is given a soporific and put painlessly out of his misery. But this is strictly voluntary, and, if he prefers to stay alive, everyone will go on treating him as kindly as ever. Officially sanctioned euthanasia is regarded as an honourable death – but if you commit suicide for reasons which the priests and the Bencheaters do not consider adequate, you forfeit all rights to either burial or cremation, and your body is just thrown unceremoniously into a pond.

Girls aren't allowed to marry until they're eighteen – boys

have to wait four years longer. Any boy or girl convicted of pre-marital intercourse is severely punished, and permanently dis-qualified from marrying, unless this sentence is remitted by the Mayor. The man and woman in charge of the household in which it happens are also publicly disgraced, for not doing their jobs properly. The Utopians are particularly strict about that kind of thing, because they think very few people would want to get married – which means spending one's whole life with the same person, and putting up with all the inconveniences that this involves – if they weren't carefully prevented from having any sexual intercourse otherwise.

When they're thinking of getting married, they do something that seemed to us quite absurd, though they take it very seriously. The prospective bride, no matter whether she's a spinster or a widow, is exhibited stark naked to the prospective bridegroom by a respectable married woman, and a suitable male chaperon shows the bridegroom naked to the bride. When we implied by our laughter that we thought it a silly system, they promptly turned the joke against *us*.

'What we find so odd,' they said, 'is the silly way these things are arranged in other parts of the world. When you're buying a horse,[26] and there's nothing at stake but a small sum of money, you take every possible precaution. The animal's practically naked already, but you firmly refuse to buy until you've whip-ped off the saddle and all the rest of the harness, to make sure there aren't any sores underneath. But when you're choosing a wife, an article that for better or worse has got to last you a lifetime, you're unbelievably careless. You don't even bother to take it out of its wrappings. You judge the whole woman from a few square inches of face, which is all you can see of her, and then proceed to marry her – at the risk of finding her most disagreeable, when you see what she's really like. No doubt you needn't worry, if moral character is the only thing that interests you – but we're not all as wise as that, and even those who are sometimes find, when they get married, that a beautiful body can be quite a useful addition to a beautiful soul. Certainly those wrappings may easily conceal enough ugliness to destroy a husband's feelings for his wife, when it's too late for a physical separation. Of course, if she turns ugly after the wedding, he

must just resign himself to his fate – but one does need some
legal protection against marriage under false pretences!'

In their case, some such precautions are particularly necessary, since unlike all their neighbours they're strictly mono-
gamous. Most married couples are parted only by death, except
in the case of adultery or intolerably bad behaviour, when the
innocent party may get permission from the Council to marry
someone else – the guilty party is disgraced, and condemned to
celibacy for life. But in no circumstances can a man divorce his
wife simply because, through no fault of her own, she has
deteriorated physically. Quite apart from the cruelty of desert-
ing a person at the very time when she most needs sympathy,
they think that, if this sort of thing were allowed, there'd be
no security whatever for old age, which not only brings many
diseases with it, but is really a disease in itself.[27]

Occasionally, though, divorce by mutual consent is allowed
on grounds of incompatibility, when both husband and wife
have found alternative partners that seem likely to make them
happier. But this requires special permission, which can only
be got after a thorough investigation by the Bencheaters and
their wives. Even then they're rather reluctant to give it, for
they think there's nothing less calculated to strengthen the
marriage tie than the prospect of easy divorce.

Adulterers are sentenced to penal servitude of the most unpleasant type. If both offenders are married, their injured partners may, if they like, obtain a divorce and marry one another,
or anyone else they choose. But if they continue to love their
undeserving mates, they're allowed to stay married to them,
provided they're willing to share their working conditions.
In such cases the Mayor is sometimes so touched by the guilty
party's remorse and the innocent party's loyalty that he lets
them both go free. But a second conviction means capital
punishment.

Otherwise there are no fixed penalties prescribed by law – the
Council decides in each case what sentence is appropriate. Husbands are responsible for punishing their wives, and parents
for punishing their children, unless the offence is so serious that
it has to be dealt with by the authorities, in the interests of
public morality. The normal penalty for any major crime is

slavery. They say it's just as unpleasant for the criminals as capital punishment, and more useful to society than getting rid of them right away, since live workers are more valuable than dead ones, and have a more prolonged deterrent effect. However, if convicts prove recalcitrant under this treatment, and don't respond to any sort of prison discipline, they're just slaughtered like wild beasts. But the prospects of those who accept the situation aren't absolutely hopeless. If, after being tamed by years of hardship, they show signs of feeling really sorry, not merely for themselves, but for what they've done, their sentence is either reduced or cancelled altogether, sometimes at the discretion of the Mayor, and sometimes by a general plebiscite.

Attempted seduction is punished no less severely than actual seduction. The same applies to every other type of offence – anyone who deliberately tries to commit a crime is legally assumed to have committed it. It's no fault of his, they argue, that he didn't bring it off, so why give him credit for his failure?

They're extremely fond of people who are mentally deficient[28] and, though it's considered very bad form to insult them, it's quite in order to find their silly behaviour amusing. In fact, it's thought better for them that you should, for, if you haven't enough sense of humour to see anything funny about the things they say and do, you're obviously not the right person to look after them. I mean, if you don't value them even as a source of entertainment, which is the only thing they're good for, you won't treat them kindly enough.

But if you start laughing at anyone who's ugly or deformed everyone will start laughing at *you*. You'll have made an awful fool of yourself by implying that people are to blame for things they can't help – for, although one's thought very lazy if one doesn't try to preserve one's natural beauty, the Utopians strongly disapprove of make-up. Actually, they've found by experience that what husbands look for in their wives is not so much physical beauty, as modesty and a respectful attitude towards themselves. A pretty face may be enough to catch a man, but it takes character and good nature to hold him.

The Utopian system includes not only deterrents from crime, but also incentives to good behaviour in the form of public honours. For instance, they put up statues in the market-place of people who've distinguished themselves by outstanding services to the community, partly to commemorate their achievements, and partly to spur on future generations to greater efforts, by reminding them of the glory of their ancestors. But anyone who deliberately tries to get himself elected to a public office is permanently disqualified from holding one. Social relations are uniformly friendly, for officials are never pompous or intimidating in their manner. They're normally addressed as 'Father', and that's how they behave. Everyone treats them with proper respect, but nobody's forced to do so. Even the Mayor himself wears perfectly ordinary clothes, without any special head-dress. His only badge of office is a bunch of corn that he carries – just as a Bishop carries[29] a taper.

They have very few laws, because, with their social system, very few laws are required. Indeed, one of their great complaints against other countries is that, although they've already got books and books of laws and interpretations of laws, they never seem to have enough. For, according to the Utopians, it's quite unjust for anyone to be bound by a legal code which is too long for an ordinary person to read right through, or too difficult for him to understand. What's more, they have no barristers to be over-ingenious about individual cases and points of law. They think it better for each man to plead his own cause, and tell the judge the same story as he'd otherwise tell his lawyer. Under such conditions, the point at issue is less likely to be obscured, and it's easier to get at the truth– for, if nobody's telling the sort of lies that one learns from lawyers, the judge can apply all his shrewdness to weighing the facts of the case, and protecting simple-minded characters against the unscrupulous attacks of clever ones.

This arrangement wouldn't work very well in other countries, because there's such a mass of complicated legislation to deal with. But in Utopia everyone's a legal expert, for the simple reason that there are, as I said, very few laws, and the crudest interpretation is always assumed to be the right one. They say the only purpose of a law is to remind people what they ought to do, so the more ingenious the interpretation, the less effective the law, since proportionately fewer people will understand it –

whereas the simple and obvious meaning stares everyone in the face. From the point of view of the lower orders, who form the largest section of the community, and are most in need of such reminders, you might just as well not make a law at all, as make one and then interpret it in a sense that can only be established after a lot of clever argument – for the ordinary person who's busy earning his living hasn't either the time or the mental capacity for that type of research.

Because of their many good qualities, the Utopians are asked by several of their neighbours to supply them with government officials, some on an annual and some on a quinquennial basis. Of course, this only happens where the people are free to make their own decisions – but the Utopians liberated most of the countries round them from dictatorships long ago. When their tour of duty expires, these officials are repatriated with every mark of honour and esteem, and replaced by other Utopians. It's certainly a very wise move on the part of the countries concerned, for the welfare of a state depends entirely on the quality of its administrators, and the Utopians are obviously ideal for the job. They can't be bribed[30] to do anything dishonest, as they'll soon be going home, where money is no use to them. And as they don't know any of the local inhabitants, they're never tempted by private likes or dislikes to make a wrong decision. These qualifications are particularly important for a judge, because personal prejudice and financial greed are the two great evils that threaten courts of law, and once they get the upper hand they immediately hamstring society, by destroying all justice.

When the Utopians talk about their 'allies' they mean these countries which they supply with administrators. 'Friendly powers' are countries that they've helped in any other way. But they never make any actual treaties of the kind that are so constantly being made, broken, and renewed by other nations. What, they ask, is the good of a treaty? Aren't all human beings natural allies already? And if a person's prepared to ignore a fundamental bond like that, is he likely to pay much attention to a mere form of words? They take this view mainly because, in their part of the world, kings aren't very scrupulous about observing pacts and agreements. In Europe, of course, especially the Christian parts of it, treaties are universally regarded as sacred and inviolate, partly because our kings are so good and just themselves, and partly because they're so much in awe of the Popes.[31] They, as we know, not only discharge their own obligations most religiously, but command all other rulers to keep their promises whatever happens, and administer stern pastoral rebukes to any who fail to do so. They evidently think, quite rightly, that it looks extremely bad for the so-called 'faithful' to break faith in such matters.

But in their part of the world, which is diametrically opposed to ours, no less in a social and moral than in a geographical sense, you can't rely on treaties at all. The more solemnly they're made, the sooner they're violated, by the simple process of discovering some loophole in the wording. Indeed, such loopholes are often incorporated deliberately in the original text, so that, no matter how binding one's commitments appear to be, one can always wriggle out of them, thus breaking both treaty and faith simultaneously. The fact is, such diplomacy is downright dishonest. If the very people who pride themselves on suggesting such tricks to their rulers found the same sort of thing going on in connexion with a private contract, they'd be the first to denounce it, in shrill, self-righteous tones, as sacrilegious and criminal. The implication seems to be that honesty is a low plebeian virtue, far beneath the dignity of royalty – or at least that there are two kinds of honesty. One is suitable for ordinary people, a plodding hack which is kept securely tethered, so that it can't go leaping any fences. The other, reserved for kings, is a far nobler animal which enjoys far greater freedom – for it's allowed to do exactly what it likes.

Anyway, that's how kings behave out there, and that, as I was saying, is presumably why the Utopians make no treaties. Perhaps if they lived in Europe they'd change their minds – though actually they disapprove of treaties on principle, however scrupulously they're observed. They say treaties make people regard one another as natural enemies. The mere fact of living on different sides of a small hill or river is supposed to sever all ties of humanity, and justify two nations in trying to destroy each other, unless there's a special treaty to forbid it. And even if there is such a treaty, it still doesn't mean that they're friends, for they always retain the right to rob one another, in so far as the drafters of the treaty have carelessly failed to include enough provisions to the contrary. The Utopians take precisely the opposite view. They think no one should be regarded as an enemy who hasn't done you any harm. Human nature constitutes a treaty in itself, and human beings are far more effectively united by kindness than by contracts, by feelings than by words.

And that brings us to the subject of war. Well, fighting is a thing they absolutely loathe. They say it's a quite subhuman[32] form of activity, although human beings are more addicted to it than any of the lower animals. In fact, the Utopians are practically the only people on earth who fail to see anything glorious in war. Of course, both sexes are given military training at regular intervals, so that they won't be incapable of fighting if they ever have to do it. But they hardly ever go to war, except in self-defence, to repel invaders from friendly territory, or to liberate the victims of dictatorship – which they do in a spirit of humanity, just because they feel sorry for them. However, they give military support to 'friendly powers', not only in defensive wars, but also in attempts to make reprisals for acts of aggression. This is always on condition that they're consulted well in advance, that they think the *casus belli* adequate, that compensation has been demanded and refused, and that the control of operations is left entirely to them. Their idea of an adequate *casus belli* includes more than robbery by force of arms. They take even stronger action to protect the rights of traders who are subjected to any kind of legal injustice in foreign countries, either as a result of unfair laws, or of fair ones deliberately misinterpreted.

That's how the war with Blindland started, a little before our time. The Utopians gave military aid to the Cloudians, because some Cloudian businessmen operating in Blindland had been the victims of some sort of legal fraud – or so the Utopians thought. Whether they were right or wrong, the result was a major war, for the bitterness of the original conflict was stepped up by the intervention of all the surrounding countries. By the time it was over, the strength of several great powers had been shattered, and others had sustained crippling losses. As for the Blindlanders, after a series of disasters they finally had to give in. The Utopians got nothing out of it – their motives were quite disinterested throughout – but the Blindlanders became the slaves of the Cloudians, who in the old days had been no match for them at all.

So you see how quick the Utopians are to avenge injuries done to their friends, even in money matters. But they're far more tolerant of injuries done to themselves. If a Utopian trader is cheated out of his goods, but suffers no physical injury, the strongest action they take is to suspend trade relations with the country concerned, until they receive compensation. Not that they care less about their own people – it's just that members of other nations are far more vulnerable to fraud, since it means the loss of their own private property, whereas a Utopian in similar circumstances loses nothing whatever. The loss is borne by the state. Besides, any goods lost are surplus to home requirements, or they'd never have been exported. So nobody feels any the worse for it – and they think it would be cruel to kill large numbers of people in revenge for something which hasn't made the slightest difference to the life or the livelihood of a single Utopian. But they take a very different line if one of their citizens is physically disabled or killed, either by a foreign government or by an individual foreigner. The moment they get news of such an incident through diplomatic channels, they immediately declare war. No form of appeasement has any effect, except the surrender of the people responsible – in which case they're sentenced to death or slavery.

They don't like bloody victories – in fact they feel ashamed of them, for they consider it stupid to pay too high a price for anything, however valuable it is. What they're really proud of is outwitting the enemy. They celebrate any success of this kind by a triumphal procession, and by putting up a trophy, as for some feat of heroism. You see, their idea of quitting themselves like men is to achieve victory by means of something which only man possesses, that is, by the power of the intellect. They say any animal can fight with its body – bears, lions, boars, wolves, dogs can all do it, and most of them are stronger and fiercer than we are – but what raises us above them is our reason and intelligence.

Their one aim in wartime is to get what they've previously failed to get by peaceful means – or, if that's out of the question, to punish the offenders so severely that nobody will ever dare to do such a thing again. They make for these objectives by the shortest possible route – but always on the principle of safety first, and national prestige second. So the moment war's declared they arrange through secret agents for lots of posters to go up simultaneously at all points on enemy territory where they're most likely to be seen. These posters carry the official seal of the Utopian government, and offer a huge reward for killing the enemy king. They also offer smaller, but still very considerable sums for killing certain individuals, whose names appear on a list, and who are presumed to be the chief supporters, after the king, of anti-Utopian policies. The reward for bringing such people in alive is twice as much as for killing them – and they themselves are offered the same amount of money, plus a free pardon, for turning against their own associates.

The immediate result is that everyone mentioned on the list becomes suspicious of everything in human shape. They all stop trusting one another, and stop being trustworthy. They live in a constant state of terror, which is perfectly justified – for it's often been known to happen that all of them, including the king himself, are betrayed by the very person that they pinned most faith on. The fact is, people will do anything for money, and there's no limit to the amount of money that the Utopians are prepared to give. Bearing in mind the risks that they're inviting each traitor to run, they're very careful to offer him compensating advantages. So, in addition to vast quantities of gold, they also promise him the freehold of a valuable estate in safe and friendly territory – and such promises they invariably keep.

This system of making take-over bids for the enemy is generally considered mean and cruel, but the Utopians are very proud of it. They say it's extremely sensible to dispose of major wars like this without fighting a single battle, and also most humane to save thousands of innocent lives at the cost of a few guilty ones. They're thinking of all the soldiers who would have been killed in action, on one side or the other – for they feel

almost as much sympathy for the mass of the enemy population
as they do for their own. They realize that these people would
never have started a war if they hadn't been forced into it by
the insanity of their rulers.

If this method fails, they sow and foster the seeds of discord among their enemies, by encouraging the king's brother
or some other member of the aristocracy to aspire to the throne.
If internal dissension shows signs of flagging, they inflame
hostility in some adjacent country by digging up one of those
ancient claims that kings are always so well provided with.
They promise to support the claimant's war effort, and do it
by supplying plenty of money and very little manpower – for
they're much too fond of one another to be willing to sacrifice
a single Utopian citizen, even in exchange for the enemy king
himself. But they're perfectly happy to hand out silver and
gold, because that's all they keep it for, and they know it
won't make any difference to their standard of living if they
spend the whole lot. Besides, quite apart from their capital
at home, they possess vast foreign assets, for, as I explained
before, a great many countries owe them money.

So most of their fighting is done by mercenaries. They recruit
them from all over the world, but especially from a place called
Venalia, which is about five hundred miles to the east of
Utopia. The Venalians[33] are extremely primitive and savage –
like the wild forests and rugged mountains among which they
grow up. They're very tough, and can stand any amount of
heat, cold, and physical hardship. They've no idea of enjoying
themselves, never do any farming, and are equally careless
about their clothes and their houses. Apart from looking after
cattle, they live mostly by hunting and stealing. In fact, they
seem naturally designed for nothing but war. They're always
looking for a war to fight in, and when they succeed in finding
one they go rushing off in their thousands to offer their services
cheap to anyone who needs soldiers. For taking lives is the
only method they know of earning a living.

They fight for their employers with great loyalty and zeal, but
won't guarantee how long they'll continue to do so. They join
you on the understanding that they'll join your enemy tomorrow, if he'll pay them better, and be back with you the

day after that, if you'll give them a little bit more. There aren't
many wars in which you won't find that most of the soldiers
on each side are Venalians. So you can imagine the sort of thing
that's always happening. Two members of a family enlist in
the same army. For a while they're the best of friends – the
next moment they're on opposite sides, and going for one
another like deadly enemies. All ties of blood and friendship are
forgotten, and they're busy cutting each other's throats. And
yet their only motive for mutual destruction is the fact that
different kings are paying them small sums of money –
and money means such a lot to them that an extra halfpenny
a day is quite enough to make them change sides. But although they yield so quickly to the temptations of avarice,
they get nothing out of it, for what they earn by bloodshed they immediately spend on debauchery of the most squalid
type.

These people will fight for the Utopians against any nation
in the world, because no one else is prepared to pay them so
much. You see, the Utopians are just as anxious to find wicked
men to exploit as good men to employ. So when necessary they
tempt Venalians with lavish promises to engage in desperate
enterprises, from which most of them never come back to claim
their earnings. But those who do are always paid in full, so
that they'll think it worth while to take similar risks in future.
For the Utopians don't care how many Venalians they send to
their deaths. They say, if only they could wipe the filthy scum
off the face of the earth completely, they'd be doing the human
race a very good turn.

Their second source of manpower is the nation for whose
benefit they've gone to war. Next come contingents supplied
by other friendly powers, and last of all their own citizens, from
whom they choose a man of proved ability to command the
combined forces. They also keep two others standing by, who
have no particular duties so long as the general is all right. But
if he's killed or taken prisoner, one of them inherits his command – and, if necessary, the other takes over from him. This
is to allow for the changing fortunes of war, and ensure that
the whole army won't become disorganized, no matter what
happens to the general.

The Utopian contingent is made up of volunteers from every town – for no one is conscripted for military service abroad. They feel that nervous people are not only unlikely to make good soldiers, but also apt to lower the morale of those around them. However, in case of invasion, able-bodied men of this type are either drafted into the navy, to serve alongside more reliable personnel, or posted at intervals on some city wall, where they've no chance of running away. When they actually come face to face with the enemy, respect for public opinion, combined with the fact that there's simply no escape, usually overcomes their fear, and in the last resort they often fight like heroes.[34]

But nobody's forced to fight overseas, and similarly no wife is forced to stay at home, if she'd rather go with her husband to the front. On the contrary, that sort of thing is much encouraged and admired. Any such wife is stationed immediately beside her husband on the battlefield, along with his children and the rest of his relations. The idea is that those who have the strongest natural instinct to help one another should be enabled to do so, by being kept as close together as possible. It's a terrible disgrace for a husband to come back without his wife, or a wife without her husband, or a child without its parents. This means that once their forces are engaged, they go on fighting to the bitter end – that is, if the enemy is prepared to stick it out. So long as they're able to wage war by proxy, the Utopians do everything they can to keep out of action, but when they're finally compelled to fight their courage is fully equal to their previous caution.

They don't fly into a fury at the first attack, but gradually, as time goes on, they grow more and more determined, until they'd rather die than yield an inch. They know there's no need to worry about food for their families, or about their children's future – two sources of anxiety that usually tend to undermine a soldier's morale – and this gives them a lofty contempt for the very idea of defeat. Their confidence is also increased by their military training. And finally they're fortified by the sound principles which they absorbed in childhood, both from their education and from their social environment. These ensure that they value life too much to throw it recklessly away, but not enough to cling on to it in a mean and cowardly manner, when it's their duty to give it up.

When the battle is at its height, a group of specially selected young men, who have sworn to stick together, try to knock out the enemy general. They keep hammering away at him by every possible method – frontal attacks, ambushes, long-range archery, hand-to-hand combat. They bear down on him in a long, unbroken wedge-formation, the point of which is constantly renewed as tired men are replaced by fresh ones. As a result, the general is nearly always killed or taken prisoner – unless he saves his skin by running away.

If the Utopians win a battle, they don't go in for any massacres. Once they've got the enemy on the run they prefer capturing to killing. They also make it a rule never to start off in pursuit, unless they can keep at least one line of troops drawn up in battle formation. They're so strict about this that, if they fail to win a battle until their rearguard goes into action, they're prepared to let the whole enemy army escape rather than establish a precedent for breaking ranks in order to pursue it. You see, they never forget a trick that they've played several times themselves. On each of these occasions the main Utopian army had been totally defeated, and the enemies were triumphantly chasing stragglers about in all directions. At this point the entire outcome of the battle was reversed by a handful of Utopians who'd been stationed in reserve. Watching for their opportunity, they suddenly counter-attacked the scattered enemy troops, who were taking no precautions, because they thought they were safe. Thus certain victory was wrested from the enemy's grasp, and the vanquished became the victors.

It's hard to say which are more cunning, their offensive or their defensive tactics. You may think they're going to retire, when it's the last thing they have in mind – and when they've really decided to do so, you'd never think it to look at them. If they feel seriously outnumbered or handicapped by the terrain, they decamp during the night without a sound, or find some other method of deluding the enemy. Or else they withdraw in daylight, but do it so gradually, and preserve such perfect formation, that they're just as dangerous to attack while retreating as while advancing.

They're always careful to fortify their camp with a very deep, broad trench, throwing the earth inside to form a rampart. For this job they don't rely on slave labour. The soldiers do it themselves, which means every soldier in the army, except for a few armed sentries who are posted in front of the rampart to watch out for emergencies. With so many hands at work, they can get a large area effectively fortified in an incredibly short time.

Their armour is strong enough to give adequate protection, but yields to every movement of the body. It doesn't even interfere with swimming – in fact they practise swimming in armour from a very early stage of their military training. Their long-range weapons are arrows, which cavalry as well as infantry learn to discharge with great force and accuracy. For close combat they use not swords but battle-axes, which because of their weight and sharpness are equally deadly for slashing or for stabbing. They also invent and manufacture most ingenious mechanical weapons, which are carefully kept out of sight until it's time to put them into action – otherwise such things are liable to be treated as a joke, and are therefore less effective. In designing this type of apparatus they concentrate particularly on making it mobile and easy to operate.

Once they've signed an armistice, they never break it, however much they're provoked. They never devastate enemy territory, or burn corn growing on it – for they regard such corn as being grown for their own benefit, so they do all they can to ensure that it's not trampled down either by their cavalry or by their infantry. They never hurt an unarmed man, unless he's a spy. They give protection to any town that surrenders, and even if they have to take it by storm they still don't loot it. They merely kill those responsible for its failure to surrender, and enslave the rest of the garrison. The whole civilian population remains untouched. Anyone known to have spoken in favour of surrender is given part of the property left by those condemned to death or slavery. The residue is presented to the allied forces – for nobody in Utopia gets any share of the spoil.

When the war's over, they send in the bill, not to the friendly powers for whose sake the expenses were incurred, but to the

defeated enemy. They demand to be paid partly in cash, which
is put aside for use in future wars, and partly in freeholds of
valuable estates on enemy territory. Thus they've acquired
property in many different countries, and the resultant income,
built up gradually from various sources, has now reached the
equivalent of more than £327,000 per annum. To each of these
countries they send out Utopian citizens, nominally to act as
rent-collectors, but actually to live there in grand style and play
the part of distinguished local residents. Still, there's plenty
of money left over to pay into the Exchequer, unless they prefer
to lend it to the country concerned, which they often do, until
such time as they actually need it themselves – and even then
they very seldom call in the whole amount. Some of these
estates they make over to individuals whom they've persuaded
to take the sort of risks that I mentioned before.

If any king goes to war with them and prepares to invade
their territory, they send off a large force to intercept him before
he reaches the frontier[35] – for they never fight on their own soil
if they can help it, and in no circumstances will they allow allied
troops to set foot on the island itself.

Finally, let me tell you about their religious ideas. There are
several different religions on the island, and indeed in each
town. There are sun-worshippers, moon-worshippers, and
worshippers of various other planets. There are people who
regard some great or good man of the past not merely as a
god, but as the supreme god. However, the vast majority take
the much more sensible view that there is a single divine power,
unknown, eternal, infinite, inexplicable, and quite beyond the
grasp of the human mind, diffused throughout this universe
of ours, not as a physical substance, but as an active force. This
power they call 'The Parent'. They give Him credit for everything that happens to everything, for all beginnings and ends,
all growth, development, and change. Nor do they recognize
any other form of deity.

On this point, indeed, all the different sects agree – that there
is one Supreme Being, Who is responsible for the creation and
management of the universe, and they all use the same Utopian word to describe Him: Mythras.[36] What they disagree about
is, who Mythras is. Some say one thing, some another – but

everyone claims that *his* Supreme Being is identical with Nature, that tremendous power which is internationally acknowledged to be the sole cause of everything. However, people are gradually tending to drift away from all these inferior creeds, and to unite in adopting what seems to be the most reasonable religion. And doubtless the others would have died out long ago if it weren't for the superstitious tendency to interpret any bad luck, when one's thinking of changing one's religion, not as a coincidence, but as a judgement from heaven – as though the discarded god were punishing one's disloyalty.

But when we told them about Christ, His teaching, His character, His miracles, and the no less miraculous devotion of all the martyrs who, by voluntarily shedding their blood, converted so many nations to the Christian faith, you've no idea how easy it was to convert them too. Perhaps they were unconsciously influenced by some divine inspiration, or perhaps it was because Christianity seemed so very like their own principal religion – though I should imagine they were also considerably affected by the information that Christ prescribed of His own disciples a communist way of life,[37] which is still practised today in all the most truly Christian communities.[38] Anyway, whatever the explanation, quite a lot of Utopians adopted our religion, and were baptized.

Unfortunately none of us four was a priest – yes, there were only four of us left – the other two had died. So though they've been admitted to all the other rites of the Church, our converts haven't yet received the sacraments that only priests can administer. But they understand about them, and want them more than anything on earth. In fact, just now they're busy discussing whether it would be in order for one of them to be ordained priest, without sending for a Christian bishop to perform the ceremony. And it certainly looked as if they were going to choose a candidate for the job, though they hadn't actually done so by the time I left.

Of course, many Utopians refuse to accept Christianity, but even they make no attempt to discourage other people from adopting it, or to attack those who do – though there was one member of our congregation who got into trouble while I was there. Immediately after his baptism, in spite of all our advice to the contrary, this man started giving public lectures on the Christian faith, in which he showed rather more zeal than discretion. Eventually he got so worked up that, not content with asserting the superiority of our religion, he went so far as to condemn all others. He kept shouting at the top of his voice that they were all vile superstitions, and that all who believed in them were monsters of impiety, destined to be punished in hell-fire for ever. When he'd been going on like this for some time, he was arrested and charged, not with blasphemy, but with disturbance of the peace. He was duly convicted and sentenced to exile – for one of the most ancient principles of their constitution is religious toleration.[39]

This principle dates right back to the time of the conquest. Up till then there'd been constant quarrels about religion, and the various warring sects had refused to cooperate in the defence of their country. When Utopos heard how they'd behaved, he realized that this was why he'd been able to conquer the whole lot of them. So immediately after his victory he made a law, by which everyone was free to practise what religion he liked, and to try and convert other people to his own faith, provided he did it quietly and politely, by rational argument. But, if he failed to convince them, he was not allowed to make bitter attacks on other religions, nor to employ violence or personal abuse. The normal penalty for being too aggressive in religious controversy is either exile or slavery.

Utopos made this law, not only to preserve the peace, which he saw being completely destroyed by endless disputes and implacable feuds, but also because he thought it was in the best interests of religion itself. He didn't presume to say which creed was right. Apparently he considered it possible that God made different people believe different things, because He wanted to be worshipped in many different ways. But he was evidently quite certain that it was stupid and arrogant to bully everyone else into adopting one's own particular creed. It seemed to him perfectly obvious that, even if there was only one true religion, and all the rest were nonsense, truth would eventually prevail of its own accord – as long as the matter was discussed calmly and reasonably. But if it was decided by force of arms, the best and most spiritual type of religion would go down before the silliest forms of superstition, just as corn is liable to be overgrown by thorns and brambles – for the worst people are always the most obstinate.

So he left the choice of creed an open question, to be decided by the individual according to his own ideas – except that he strictly and solemnly forbade his people to believe anything so incompatible with human dignity as the doctrine that the soul dies with the body, and the universe functions aimlessly, without any controlling providence. That's why they feel so sure that there must be rewards and punishments after death. Anyone who thinks differently has, in their view, forfeited his right to be classed as a human being, by degrading his immortal soul to the level of an animal's body. Still less do they regard him as a Utopian citizen. They say a person like that doesn't really care a damn for the Utopian way of life – only he's too frightened to say so. For it stands to reason, if you're not afraid of anything but prosecution, and have no hopes of anything after you're dead, you'll always be trying to evade or break the laws of your country, in order to gain your own private ends. So nobody who subscribes to this doctrine is allowed to receive any public honour, hold any public appointment, or work in any public service. In fact such people are generally regarded as utterly contemptible.

They're not punished in any way, though, for no one is held responsible for what he believes. Nor are they terrorized into concealing their views, because Utopians simply can't stand hypocrisy, which they consider practically equivalent to fraud. Admittedly, it's illegal for any such person to argue in defence of his beliefs, but that's only in public. In private discussions with priests or other serious-minded characters, he's not merely allowed but positively encouraged to do so, for everyone's convinced that this type of delusion will eventually yield to reason.

Indeed there are some Utopians – quite a lot of them actually – who, so far from being materialists, go to the opposite extreme. Of course, there's no law against them, for they have a certain amount of reason on their side, and are quite decent characters in themselves. These people believe that animals have immortal souls too, though much inferior to ours, and designed for happiness on a lower plane. As for the infinite happiness in store for human beings, practically everyone feels so sure of it that, although they always mourn for an illness, they never mourn for a death – unless the person in question was obviously uneasy and unwilling to let go of life. This they regard as a very bad sign. It seems to suggest that the soul is conscious of its own guilt, and has gloomy forebodings of punishment to come – hence its terror of dying. Besides, they doubt if God will be at all pleased to see someone who, instead of running gladly to answer His summons, has to be dragged into His presence by force. So they shudder to see a death of this type, and perform the funeral rites in sorrowful silence. They merely say, 'God have mercy on his soul, and forgive his weaknesses.' Then they bury the body.

But when a person dies in a cheerful and optimistic mood,[40] nobody mourns for him. They sing for joy at his funeral, and lovingly commend his soul to God. Finally, more in a spirit of reverence than of grief, they cremate the body, and mark the spot by a column engraved with an epitaph. Then they go home and discuss the dead man's character and career, and there's nothing in his life that they dwell on with such pleasure as the happy state of mind in which he left it. This method of recalling his good qualities is thought the best way of encouraging similar virtues in the living, and also of pleasing the dead – for the subject of these discussions is believed to be present at them, though invisible to human eyes. After all, perfect happiness implies complete freedom of movement, and no one with any feeling would stop wanting to see his friends when he died, if they'd been really fond of one another while he was alive. On the contrary, the Utopians assume that a good man's capacity for affection, like every other good thing about him, is increased rather than diminished by death. So they believe that the dead mix freely with the living, and observe everything they say and do. In fact they regard them almost as guardian angels, and this gives them greater confidence in tackling all their problems. Also, the sense of their ancestors' presence discourages any bad behaviour in private.

They pay no attention to omens, fortune-telling, or any of the superstitious practices that are taken so seriously in other countries. In fact they treat them as a joke. But they have a great respect for miracles which aren't attributable to natural causes, because they see them as evidence of God's presence and power. They say such miracles often happen there. Indeed at moments of crisis the whole country prays for a miracle, and their faith is so great that the prayer is sometimes answered.

Most Utopians feel they can please God merely by studying the natural world, and praising Him for it. But quite a lot of them are led by their religion to neglect the pursuit of knowledge. They're not interested in science – they simply have no time for that sort of thing, since they believe that the only way to earn happiness after death is to spend one's life doing good works. Some of them look after invalids, while others mend roads, clean out ditches, repair bridges, dig up turf, sand, or stone, cut down and saw up trees, or cart such things as timber and corn into the towns. In short, they behave like servants, and work harder than slaves, not only for the community, but also for private individuals. They cheerfully undertake all the rough, dirty, and difficult jobs that the average person fights shy of, either because of the physical effort involved, or just because he dislikes them, or despairs of ever getting them done. Thus they create leisure for other people by working ceaselessly themselves – and yet they take no credit for it. They never find fault with other ways of life, or boast about their own. So the more they make slaves of themselves, the more everybody respects them.

They're divided into two sects, of which one believes in celibacy. Its members are total abstainers, not only from sexual intercourse, but also from meat, and in some cases from every form of animal food. They renounce all the pleasures of this life, which they regard as sinful, and yearn only for the life to come. This they try to earn by the sweat of their brows, and by going without sleep – but the hope of reaching it any day now keeps them lively and cheerful. The other sect, though equally keen on hard work, approves of marriage, on the grounds that its comforts are not to be despised, and that procreation is a duty which one owes to both nature and to one's country. They have no objection to pleasure, so long as it doesn't interfere with work. On that principle they eat a lot of meat, because they think it enables them to work harder. They're generally considered more sensible than the others, though the others are thought more devout. Of course, if the members of the first sect tried to justify their behaviour on logical grounds, they'd merely be laughed at. But as they admit that their motives are religious rather than rational, they're regarded with great reverence – for Utopians are always extremely careful to avoid rash judgements in the matter of religion. People who belong to this sect are known in their own language as Cowparsons⁴¹ which may be roughly translated, Lay Brethren.

All their priests are exceptionally pious, which means that there are very few of them – normally thirteen per town, or one per church. But in wartime seven of the thirteen go off with the troops, and seven more priests are ordained as temporary substitutes. When the army chaplains return, they get back their old livings, and the extra priests remain on the staff of the Bishop – for one of the thirteen is given this status – until they succeed, one by one, to vacancies created by the death of the original incumbents.

Priests are elected by the whole community. The election is by secret ballot, as it is for all public appointments, to prevent the formation of pressure groups, and the successful candidates are then ordained by their colleagues. Priests are responsible for conducting services, organizing religions, and supervising morals. It's considered very shameful to be had up before an ecclesiastical court, or even reprimanded by a priest for bad behaviour. Of course, the actual suppression and punishment of crime is the job of the Mayor and other public officials. Priests merely give advice and warning – though they can also excommunicate persistent offenders, and there's hardly any punishment that people fear more. You see, a person who has been excommunicated is not only completely disgraced and racked with fears of divine vengeance. His physical security is threatened too, for, unless he can very soon convince the priests that he's a reformed character, he's arrested and punished by the Council for impiety.

Priests are also responsible for the education of children and adolescents, in which quite as much stress is laid on moral as on academic training. They do their utmost to ensure that, while

children are still at an impressionable age, they're given the
right ideas about things – the sort of ideas best calculated to
preserve the structure of their society. If thoroughly absorbed
in childhood, these ideas will persist throughout adult life, and
so contribute greatly to the safety of the state, which is never
seriously threatened except by moral defects arising from wrong
ideas.

Male priests are allowed to marry[42] – for there's nothing to
stop a woman from becoming a priest,[43] although women
aren't often chosen for the job, and only elderly widows are
eligible. As a matter of fact, clergymen's wives form the cream
of Utopian society,[44] for no public figure is respected more
than a priest. So much so that, even if a priest commits a crime,
he's not liable to prosecution. They just leave him to God and
his own conscience, since, no matter what he has done, they
don't think it right for any human being to lay hands on a man
who has been dedicated as a special offering to God. They find
this rule quite easy to keep, because priests represent such a tiny
minority, and because they're so carefully chosen. After all, it's
not really very likely that a man who has come out top of a list
of excellent candidates, and who owes his appointment entirely
to his moral character, should suddenly become vicious and
corrupt. And even if we must accept that possibility – human
nature being so very unpredictable – a mere handful of people
without any executive power can hardly constitute a serious
danger to the community. They keep the numbers down, in
order not to lower the present high prestige of the priest-
hood, by making the honour less of a rarity – especially as
they say it's hard to find many people suitable for a
profession which demands considerably more than average
virtues.

The reputation of Utopian priests is just as good abroad as it
is at home. The evidence and, I think, the reason for this may be
found in what happens on the battlefield. While the fighting is
in progress, the priests kneel a short way off, wearing their
holy vestments, and hold up their hands to heaven. They pray
first for peace, and then for a bloodless victory – bloodless on
both sides. As soon as their own troops start getting the best of
it, the priests hurry on to the battlefield and stop all unnecessary

violence. Once they appear on the scene, an enemy soldier can save his life simply by calling out to them, and, if he can manage to touch their flowing robes, his property too is safe from any sort of war damage. This earns them so much respect in every country, and gives them so much genuine authority, that they've often been able to protect their own soldiers quite as effectively as they normally protect the enemy's. Sometimes, at desperate moments when the Utopian forces are in full retreat, and their enemies were rushing after them, intent on killing and looting, the intervention of the priests has been known to prevent a massacre, part the combatants, and bring about the conclusion of a peace on equal terms. For the person of a Utopian priest is universally regarded as sacred and inviolable even among the most savage and barbarous nations.

They have religious festivals on the first and last days of each month, and also of each year – their calendar, by the way, is based on the solar year, divided into lunar months. These first days are called Dogdates in their language, and the last ones Turndates – in other words, Beginning Feasts and Ending Feasts.

Their churches look most impressive, not only because they're so beautifully built, but also because of their size. You see, as there are so few of them, they have to be capable of holding vast numbers of people. However, they're all rather dark, which is not, I'm told, a mistake on the part of the architects, but a matter of policy. The priests think that too much light tends to distract one's attention, whereas a sort of twilight helps one to collect one's thoughts, and intensifies religious feeling. Now this doesn't take the same form with everyone, though all its varieties lead by different routes, as it were, to the same destination: the worship of the Divine Being. For that reason, there's nothing to be seen or heard in their churches which can't equally well be applied to all religions. Any ceremonies which are peculiar to individual sects are performed privately at home, and public services are so arranged as not to detract in any way from these private ones.

On the same principle, their churches contain no visual representations of God, so that everyone's left free to imagine Him in whatever shape he chooses, according to which religion he thinks the best. Nor is God addressed by any special names there. He is simply called Mythras, a general term used by everybody to designate the Supreme Being, whoever He may be. Similarly, no prayers are said in which each member of the congregation cannot join without prejudice to his own particular creed.

At Ending Feasts they fast all day, and go to church in the evening, to thank God for bringing them safely to the end of the year or month in question. Next day, which is of course a Beginning Feast, they meet at church in the morning to pray for happiness and prosperity during the year or month which has just begun. But before going to church at an Ending Feast, wives kneel down at home before their husbands, and children before their parents, to confess all their sins of omission and commission, and ask to be forgiven. This gets rid of any little grudges that may have clouded the domestic atmosphere, so that everyone can attend divine service with an absolutely clear mind. To do so when one is feeling upset is thought positively blasphemous. For that reason, anyone who's conscious of feeling anger or resentment towards another person stays away from church until he's made it up, and purged himself of these unpleasant emotions, for fear of being promptly and severely punished otherwise.

As they enter the church, the men turn to the right and the women to the left, and the seating is so arranged that the males of each household are in front of the house-father, and the house-mother acts as a rearguard for the females. This ensures that everyone's conduct in public is watched by those who are responsible for his discipline at home. Here too they take great care to see that a young person always sits next to an older one – for if children are left to themselves they're apt to waste their time in church playing childish games, when they ought above all to be developing a sense of religious awe, the strongest, if not the only incentive to good behaviour.

They never sacrifice any animals, for they can't imagine a merciful God enjoying slaughter and bloodshed. They say God gave His creatures life, because He wanted them to live. But they do make certain burnt offerings – of incense and other aromatic substances, and of innumerable candles. Of course they realize that such things are no use to the Divine Being, but they see no harm in them as a form of tribute, and feel that these scents and lights and other elements of ritual somehow raise people's thoughts, and make them more eager to worship God.

The congregation is dressed in white, and the priest wears multi-coloured vestments, magnificent in workmanship and design, but made of quite cheap materials – for instead of being woven with gold thread, or encrusted with rare jewels, they're merely decorated with the feathers[45] of various birds. On the other hand, their value as works of art is far greater than that of the richest material in the world. Besides, the feathers are arranged in special patterns which are said to symbolize certain divine truths, and the priests are careful to teach the meaning of these hieroglyphics, since they serve to remind worshippers of God's favours towards them, of their duty towards Him in return, and of their duty towards one another.

The moment the priest appears from the sanctuary wearing these vestments, everyone bows down to the ground in reverence, and there is deep silence throughout the building. The effect is so awe-inspiring that one almost seems to feel a divine presence. After a few minutes the priest gives a sign for the congregation to stand up. Then they sing hymns of praise to God, accompanied by musical instruments, which are generally quite different from anything to be seen in our part of the world. Most of these have a much sweeter tone than ours, though some of them simply won't bear comparison with European instruments. But in one respect they're undoubtedly far ahead of us. All their music, both vocal and instrumental, is wonderfully expressive of natural feelings. The sound is so well adapted to the sense that whether the theme is prayer or rejoicing, agitation or calm, sorrow or anger, the melodic line exactly represents the appropriate emotion. It therefore enters deeply into the hearer's consciousness, and has an extraordinarily stimulating effect.

The service ends with a set form of prayer repeated by both priests and congregation. It's worded in such a way that, while they're all saying it together, each person can apply it to himself. It goes something like this:

O God, I acknowledge Thee to be my creator, my governor, and
the source of all good things. I thank Thee for all Thy blessings, but
especially for letting me live in the happiest possible society, and
practise what I hope is the truest religion. If I am wrong, and if
some other religion or social system would be better and more
acceptable to Thee, I pray Thee in Thy goodness to let me know it,
for I am ready to follow wherever Thou shalt lead me. But if our
system is indeed the best, and my religion the truest, then keep me
faithful to both of them, and bring the rest of humanity to adopt the
same way of life, and the same religious faith – unless the present
variety of creeds is part of Thy inscrutable purpose. Grant me an easy
death, when Thou takest me to Thyself. I do not presume to suggest
whether it should be late or soon. But if it is Thy will, I would much
rather come to Thee by a most painful death, than be kept too long
away from Thee by the most pleasant of earthly lives.

After saying this prayer, they again bow down to the
ground for a few moments, and then get up and go off to
lunch. The rest of the day is spent in recreation and military
training.

Well, that's the most accurate account I can give you of the
Utopian Republic. To my mind, it's not only the best country
in the world, but the only one that has any right to call itself a
republic.[46] Elsewhere, people are always talking about the
public interest, but all they really care about is private property.
In Utopia, where there's no private property, people take their
duty to the public seriously. And both attitudes are perfectly
reasonable. In other 'republics' practically everyone knows
that, if he doesn't look out for himself, he'll starve to death,
however prosperous his country may be. He's therefore compelled to give his own interests priority over those of the public;
that is, of other people. But in Utopia, where everything's under
public ownership, no one has any fear of going short, as long
as the public storehouses are full. Everyone gets a fair share, so
there are never any poor men or beggars. Nobody owns anything, but everyone is rich – for what greater wealth can there
be than cheerfulness, peace of mind, and freedom from anxiety?
Instead of being worried about his food supply, upset by the
plaintive demands of his wife, afraid of poverty for his son, and
baffled by the problem of finding a dowry for his daughter, the

Utopian can feel absolutely sure that he, his wife, his children, his grandchildren, his great-grandchildren, and as long a line of descendants as the proudest peer could wish to look forward to, will always have enough to eat and enough to make them happy. There's also the further point that those who are too old to work are just as well provided for as those who are still working.

Now, will anyone venture to compare these fair arrangements in Utopia with the so-called justice of other countries? – in which I'm damned if I can see the slightest trace of justice or fairness. For what sort of justice do you call this? People like aristocrats, goldsmiths, or money-lenders, who either do no work at all, or do work that's really not essential, are rewarded for their laziness or their unnecessary activities by a splendid life of luxury. But labourers, coachmen, carpenters, and farm-hands, who never stop working like cart-horses, at jobs so essential that, if they *did* stop working, they'd bring any country to a standstill within twelve months – what happens to them? They get so little to eat, and have such a wretched time, that they'd be almost better off if they *were* cart-horses. Then at least, they wouldn't work quite such long hours, their food wouldn't be very much worse, they'd enjoy it more, and they'd have no fears for the future. As it is, they're not only ground down by unrewarding toil in the present, but also worried to death by the prospect of a poverty-stricken old age – since their daily wages aren't enough to support them for one day, let alone leave anything over to be saved up when they're old.

Can you see any fairness or gratitude in a social system which lavishes such great rewards on so-called noblemen, goldsmiths, and people like that, who are either totally unproductive or merely employed in producing luxury goods[47] or entertainment, but makes no such kind provision for farm-hands, coal-heavers, labourers, carters, or carpenters, without whom society couldn't exist at all? And the climax of ingratitude comes when they're old and ill and completely destitute. Having taken advantage of them throughout the best years of their lives, society now forgets all the sleepless hours they've spent in its service, and repays them for all the vital work they've done, by letting them die in misery. What's more, the wretched earnings of the poor are daily whittled away by the rich, not only through private dishonesty, but through public legislation. As if it weren't unjust enough already that the man who contributes most to society should get the least in return, they make it even worse, and then arrange for injustice to be legally described as justice.[48]

In fact, when I consider any social system that prevails in the modern world, I can't, so help me God, see it as anything but a conspiracy of the rich to advance their own interests under the pretext of organizing society. They think up all sorts of tricks and dodges, first for keeping safe their ill-gotten gains, and then for exploiting the poor by buying their labour as cheaply as possible. Once the rich have decided that these tricks and dodges shall be officially recognized by society – which includes the poor as well as the rich – they acquire the force of law. Thus an unscrupulous minority is led by its insatiable greed to monopolize what would have been enough to supply the needs of the whole population. And yet how much happier even these people would be in Utopia! There, with the simultaneous abolition of money and the passion for money, how many other social problems have been solved, how many crimes eradicated! For obviously the end of money means the end of all those types of criminal behaviour which daily punishments are powerless to check: fraud, theft, burglary, brawls, riots, disputes, rebellion, murder, treason, and black magic.[49] And the moment money goes, you can also say good-bye to fear, tension, anxiety, overwork, and sleepless nights. Why, even poverty itself, the one problem that has always seemed to need money for its solution, would promptly disappear if money ceased to exist.

Let me try to make this point clearer. Just think back to one of the years when the harvest was bad, and thousands of people died of starvation. Well, I bet if you'd inspected every rich man's barn at the end of that lean period you'd have found enough corn to have saved all the lives that were lost through malnutrition and disease, and prevented anyone from suffering any ill effects whatever from the meanness of the weather and the soil. Everyone could so easily get enough to eat, if it weren't for that blessed nuisance, money. There you have a brilliant invention which was designed to make food more readily available. Actually it's the only thing that makes it unobtainable.

I'm sure that even the rich are well aware of all this, and realize how much better it would be to have everything one needed, than lots of things one didn't need – to be evacuated altogether from the danger area, than to dig oneself in behind a barricade of enormous wealth. And I've no doubt that either self-interest, or the authority of our Saviour Christ – Who was far too wise not to know what was best for us, and far too kind to recommend anything else – would have led the whole world to adopt the Utopian system long ago, if it weren't for that beastly root of all evils, pride. For pride's criterion of prosperity is not what you've got yourself, but what other people haven't got. Pride would refuse to set foot in paradise, if she thought there'd be no under-privileged classes there to gloat over and order about – nobody whose misery could serve as a foil to her own happiness, or whose poverty she could make harder to bear, by flaunting her own riches. Pride, like a hellish serpent gliding through human hearts – or shall we say, like a sucking-fish[50] that clings to the ship of state? – is always dragging us back, and obstructing our progress towards a better way of life.

But as this fault is too deeply ingrained in human nature to be easily eradicated, I'm glad that at least one country has managed to develop a system which I'd like to see universally adopted. The Utopian way of life provides not only the happiest basis for a civilized community, but also one which, in all human probability, will last for ever. They've eliminated the root-causes of ambition, political conflict, and everything like that. There's therefore no danger of internal dissension, the one thing that has destroyed so many impregnable towns. And as long as there's unity and sound administration at home, no matter how envious neighbouring kings may feel, they'll never be able to shake, let alone to shatter, the power of Utopia. They've tried to do so often enough in the past, but have always been beaten back.

While Raphael was telling us all this, I kept thinking of

various objections. The laws and customs of that country seemed to me in many cases perfectly ridiculous. Quite apart from such things as their military tactics, religions, and forms of worship, there was the grand absurdity on which their whole society was based, communism minus money. Now this in itself would mean the end of the aristocracy, and consequently of all dignity, splendour, and majesty, which are generally supposed to be the real glories of any nation.

However, I could see that he was tired after talking so much, and I was not quite sure how tolerant he would be of any opinion that contradicted his own – especially when I remembered his sarcastic reference to the sort of person who is afraid of looking a fool if he cannot pick holes in other people's ideas. So I just made some polite remarks about the Utopian system, and thanked him for his interesting talk – after which I took his arm and led him in to supper, saying:

'Well, I must think it over. Then perhaps we can meet again and discuss it at greater length.'

I certainly hope we shall, some day. In the meantime I cannot agree with everything that he said, for all his undoubted learning and experience. But I freely admit that there are many features of the Utopian Republic which I should like – though I hardly expect – to see adopted in Europe.[51]

NOTES

INTRODUCTION

1. *John Aubrey has a story:* Sir William Roper, of Eltham, in Kent, came one morning, pretty early, to my Lord, with a proposal to marry one of his daughters. My Lord's daughters were then both together abed in a truckle-bed in their father's chamber asleep. He carries Sir William into the chamber and takes the sheet by the corner and suddenly whips it off. They lay on their backs, and their smocks up as high as their armpits. This awakened them, and immediately they turned on their bellies. Quoth Roper, I have seen both sides, and so gave a pat on the buttock he made choice of, saying, Thou art mine. Here was all the trouble of the wooing. This account I had from my honoured friend old Mrs Tyndale, whose grandfather, Sir William Stafford, was an intimate friend of this Sir W. Roper, who told him the story. (*Brief Lives,* unpublished at Aubrey's death in 1697; here quoted from edition by O. L. Dick, London, 1950. I have modernized the spelling, as in all quotations from authors employing obsolete orthography.)

2. *Epigrammata . . . No. 149:* omitted from the collected Latin works (1565), presumably because Germain de Brie (with whom More had a literary dispute) pointed out a mistake in the scansion of one line.

3. *Utopos . . . dramme pagloni:* The lines are evidently intended to be scanned as hexameters.

4. *Utopos me General:* the title, *dux,* appears to be a military one, though it could also be interpreted as *Fuehrer.* There is no justification in the text of *Utopia* for calling the eponymous conqueror a king, as Robinson does.

5. *without philosophy State philosophical:* the idea seems to be that although Utopia does not (like ancient Greece, for instance) go in for much abstract philosophizing, it has realized in practice a philosophical ideal.

6. *The Poet Laureate, Mr Windbag:* it has been suggested that this is a hit at John Skelton (1460?–1529), who was 'poet laureate' of Oxford and Cambridge Universities; I have therefore assumed that Nonsenso's sister married an Englishman.

7. *NOPLACIA . . . GOPLACIA:* the original pun is on *Utopia* (not-place) and *Eutopia* (well-place).

MORE'S LETTER TO PETER GILLES

8. *Peter Gilles* or Gillis (*Aegidius* in the Latin text) was born at Antwerp in 1486 and died there in 1533. He became Chief Secretary of Antwerp in 1510, and edited several books, including Aesop's fables. He was a friend of Erasmus, who introduced him to More in 1515.

9. *in the law courts:* in addition to his private practice, he was Under-Sheriff of London (i.e. the Sheriff's legal adviser). His son-in-law, William Roper, confirms how busy he was: 'There was at that time in none of the Prince's courts of the laws of this realm, any matter of importance in controversy wherein he was not with the one part of Counsel.' (*Life*, London, 1935, p. 9.)

10. *John Clement* (died 1572) was educated at St Paul's School, and then taken into More's household, as a tutor to his children, one of whom (his adopted daughter, Margaret Gigs) Clement married in 1526. He became a Reader in Greek at Oxford, then studied medicine and eventually became Queen Mary's physician.

11. *a very pious theologian:* according to the 1624 edition of Robinson's translation, this was thought by some people to be Dr Rowland Philips, Vicar of Croydon (died 1538?).

12. *begging for preferment:* in Utopia 'anyone who deliberately tries to get himself elected to a public office is permanently disqualified from holding one' (p. 106).

GILLES'S LETTER TO BUSLEIDEN

13. *Busleiden:* Jerome Busleiden (about 1470–1517) is here addressed as 'Provost of Aire, and Councillor of the Catholic King Charles', i.e. Prince Charles of Castile, later the Emperor Charles V, but then King of the Netherlands. Busleiden was also Archdeacon of Cambrai and of Brussels, and by his will the founder of the Collegium Trilingue (for the teaching of Greek, Latin, and Hebrew) at Louvain. More met him in 1515.

14. *marginal notes:* mostly paragraph headings, though they occasionally explain allusions, point contrasts between Utopian and European habits, exclaim briefly at good passages ('marvellous simile!' or 'delightful story!'), or administer the equivalent of an elbow in the ribs: 'Notice that, reader!'

BOOK ONE

1. *a rather serious difference of opinion:* a marriage had been arranged between Henry VIII's sister, Princess Mary, and Prince Charles of Castile. The engagement was broken off by Prince Charles because he thought it would be more to his interest to form an alliance with Francis I of France, by getting engaged to his sister-in-law Renée (who was then four years old). By way of reprisals, the English Government prohibited the export of wool to Prince Charles's dominions in the Netherlands; but, as this was found to have an adverse effect on the English wool trade, a legation was sent to Flanders to re-open commercial relations. More was put on it (7 May 1515) at the request of the English merchants. He wrote the second book of *Utopia* during his six-months' stay in the Netherlands: the first was written after his return to England.

2. *Cuthbert Tunstall* (1474–1559) became Bishop of London in 1522, and Bishop of Durham in 1529. He inadvertently gave financial support to the Protestants, by buying up a great many copies of Tyndale's translation of the New Testament, in order to burn them. He wrote a book on arithmetic, which he dedicated to More, and received another glowing testimonial in More's epitaph.

3. *labour the obvious:* the original has, *solem lucerna, quod aiunt, ostendere* (to show the sun, as they say, with a lamp); but, in the absence of a similar English proverbial expression, I have jettisoned the imagery.

4. *over one shoulder:* according to Roger Ascham (1515–68) this was one of More's own mannerisms.

5. *Palinurus:* the pilot of Aeneas, who went to sleep at the helm, fell into the sea, swam ashore, and was murdered by the local inhabitants (*Aeneid,* v, 833–71; vi, 349–62). The point seems to be that Palinurus was a professional sailor, not a philosophical explorer, and was not an outstandingly wide-awake type.

6. *Raphael Nonsenso:* for the meaning of the name, see Introduction (p. 8).

7. *Amerigo Vespucci* (1451–1512) was a Florentine merchant from whom America was named, on the strength of his claim (not substantiated) to have discovered 'Terra Firma', i.e. the mainland of South America, during a voyage made in 1497. More may have got some hints for *Utopia* from Vespucci's *New World* (Basel, about 1505) recording what he saw on a voyage begun in 1501. This pamphlet describes people who 'have no private property, but everything is shared in common. They live together without a king, with-

out a government, and everyone is his own master ... They live according to nature, and may be called Epicureans rather than Stoics ... The natives said that there was a great deal of gold inland, and that it was not prized or considered of any value there.' However, they differ from the Utopians more sensationally than they resemble them. They are, for example, cannibals, who eat prisoners of war, and occasionally their own wives and children: Vespucci spoke to a man reputed to have eaten more than 300 human bodies. They also go around stark naked, and the women have a special method of making their husbands' private parts swell up to a monstrous size (by getting a certain poisonous animal to bite them).

8. *Four Voyages:* first published in *Cosmographiae Introductio,* St Dié 1507. The First Voyage contains a description of some natives who have several points in common with the Utopians. They have no iron (p. 48); their houses belong equally to everyone, and they change houses every seven or eight years (p. 52); they utterly despise gold, pearls, and jewels (p. 53). They also take their wives with them when they go to war; not, however, as warriors but as a form of transport for 'one of their women can put more on her back, and then carry it for thirty or forty leagues (as we often saw for ourselves) than even a strong man can lift from the ground.' (pp. 48-9)

9. *that fort:* in his *Four Voyages* (1507) Vespucci relates that in 1504 he left twenty-four men, with arms and provisions for six months, in a fort built at a place which has since been identified as Cape Frio.

10. *The unburied . . . sky:* Lucan, *Pharsalia,* VII, 819.

11. *You can . . . anywhere:* 'When Anaxagoras was dying at Lampsacus, his friends asked him if he wanted to be taken home to Clazomenae, in case anything happened to him; to which he made the splendid answer, "That will be quite unnecessary – you can get to the Underworld from anywhere."' (Cicero, *Tusculanae Disputationes,* I, 104).

More made a similar reply, when his wife visited him in the Tower, and called him a fool for voluntarily leaving his comfortable home and living in 'this close, filthy prison': 'Is not this house . . . as nigh heaven as my own?' (Roper, *Life,* p. 83.)

12. *horrible creatures . . . whole populations:* the original has 'Scyllas and Celaenos and people-devouring Lestrigonians'. Scylla is a six-headed monster in the *Odyssey* (XII, 235–59) who snatches and eats six members of Odysseus's crew; Celaeno is one of the Harpies in the *Aeneid* (III, 211ff.), woman-faced birds of prey, who snatch food away, just as one is going to eat it; the Lestrigonians are cannibalistic giants in the *Odyssey* (X, 105ff.). It seems to me that, in the context,

these monsters are used as symbols for those who prey upon society, and I have translated accordingly.

13. PETER: to avoid peppering the page with inverted commas, when More is describing a conversation, in which Raphael is describing a conversation, in which two speakers quote passages from the Bible, I have borrowed from the novels of T. L. Peacock the trick of supplementing quotation marks with the notation normally used for dramatic dialogue.

14. *service of some king:* the discussion that follows is probably a dramatization of an internal conflict that More was experiencing at the time. On 17 February 1516 he mentioned in a letter to Erasmus that he had refused a pension from the King; on 25 October he wrote that Erasmus was wise to avoid being mixed up in 'the busy trifles of princes'; but some time during the first three months of 1518 he decided to join the royal service, and entered on a public career which culminated in his becoming Lord Chancellor in 1529.

15. *a revolution:* in 1497 the people of Cornwall rebelled, under the leadership of a lawyer called Thomas Flammock, against the imposition of taxes to pay for an invasion of Scotland. They collected a force of 15,000 men, who were finally defeated at Blackheath on 17 June. Two thousand of them were killed in the battle.

16. *John Morton:* the passage is semi-autobiographical, for More was brought up from the age of twelve in Morton's household. 'In whose wit and towardness the Cardinal much delighting, would often say of him unto the nobles that divers times dined with him: "This child here waiting at table, whosoever shall live to see it, will prove a marvellous man."' (W. Roper, *Life*, London, 1935, p. 5.)

17. *fighting in France:* in October 1492 an English force landed at Calais, and ineffectually besieged Boulogne, in fulfilment of Henry VII's treaty obligations.

18. *Sallust: Catilina,* xvi.

19. *the poor creatures:* in 1529 some of More's barns were burned down, and in a letter to his wife he raised the question of selling the land, but continued: 'I think it were not best suddenly thus to leave it all up, and to put away our folk of our farm, till we have somewhat advised us thereon. Howbeit, if we have more now than ye shall need, and which can get them other masters, ye may then discharge us of them. But I would not that any man were suddenly sent away he wot ne'er whither.' (*English Works*, 1557, p. 1419D.)

20. *clothes of a special colour:* there is a marginal note: 'Nowadays noblemen's servants actually pride themselves on being dressed like that.'

21. *Ye shall . . . patience:* Luke, xxi, 19.

22. *Be ye . . . sin not:* Psalms, iv, 4 (Vulgate and Septuagint). The Revised Version has, 'Be angry, but sin not', and the Authorized, 'Stand in awe, and sin not'.

23. *The zeal . . . me up:* Psalms, lxix, 9.

24. *They who . . . punished:* from the Easter Hymn of Adam of St Victor (died between 1172 and 1192; *Oeuvres,* edited by L. Gautier, I, pp. 89–90, Paris, 1858). The reference is to the story of Elisha (II Kings, ii, 23–4) who was jeered at by some children for being bald. He cursed them so effectively that forty-two of them were torn to pieces by bears. Through ignorance or rage the friar makes a grammatical mistake in his quotation (treating the second declension masculine noun *zelus* as though it were a third declension neuter); so I have done equal violence to English syntax.

25. *Answer . . . folly:* Proverbs, xxvi, 5.

26. *what . . . Plato says: Republic,* v, 473d.

27. *Dionysius:* dictator of Syracuse 405–367 B.C. He was introduced to Plato, but was unimpressed by his doctrines, and is said to have had him sold into slavery at the end of one of his visits to Syracuse.

28. *the following problems:* they seem largely based on the activities of Louis XII and Francis I. Immediately on his succession, Louis took the title of Duke of Milan. In February 1499 he made a pact with Venice, and his troops entered Milan on 6 October. In November 1500 he made a treaty with Aragon for the joint conquest of Naples, which he occupied on 4 August 1501. In December 1508 he joined the League of Cambrai, an alliance with Pope Julius II, the Emperor Maximilian I, and Ferdinand of Aragon, against Venice, on which he then declared war (7 April 1509). In 1515 he was succeeded by Francis, who at once took steps to reconquer Milan (it had been wrested away from France two years before), by invading Italy and defeating an army of Swiss mercenaries at Marignano on 13 September of the same year.

29. *Navarre:* from 1234 onwards Navarre was in the hands of French kings, though it was claimed by the kings of Aragon. In 1515 Ferdinand the Catholic, King of Aragon and Castile, assumed the title of King of Navarre, and the next year finally annexed Spanish Navarre.

30. *exiled English nobleman:* possibly a reference to Perkin Warbeck (1474–99), who claimed to be Duke of York. He was encouraged by Charles VIII of France, and was with James IV of Scotland when he invaded England in September 1496.

31. *raising . . . currency:* both Edward IV and Henry VII raised the value of the noble, but in the first case the motive was the need to compete with foreign mints for bullion, and, in the second, the need

to prevent English currency from draining away to Europe, in view of the debasement of continental currencies. It was not until 1544 that English coinage seems to have been debased, purely as a royal expedient for making money out of the English people.

32. *pretend to start a war:* perhaps an allusion to 1492, when Henry VII raised a special levy to pay for the war against France, and on 3 November of the same year made peace by the Treaty of Étaples, under which Charles VIII agreed to pay him 50,000 francs a year.

33. *third ... fourth:* these methods of increasing revenue were freely used by Henry VII, with the help of his agents, Empson and Dudley.

34. *Crassus:* Marcus Licinius Crassus (died 53 B.C.), member of the First Triumvirate with Pompey and Julius Caesar. He was a bold financier who built up a vast fortune by such practices as buying houses cheap when they were on fire, or threatened by fire, until finally he owned most of Rome. The 'doctrine' mentioned here seems to be based on a sentence in Pliny (*Natural History*, xxxiii, 10): 'M. Crassus used to say that no one was rich who could not support a legion out of his annual income.'

35. *kind ... seize it:* in 1504 More, as a young M.P., made himself unpopular with Henry VII by obstructing his demand for about £90,000. 'It is clear from the *Rolls* that Parliament raised difficulties; in the end the King had to be satisfied with a grant of £40,000, and thought well to meet his subjects by, "of his ample grace and pity", remitting a quarter of that.' (R. W. Chambers, *Thomas More*, p. 87.) He then worked off his resentment against More by trumping up some charge against his father, and keeping him in the Tower until he paid a fine of £100.

36. *Fabricius:* Gaius Fabricius Luscinus (early third century B.C.), famous for his integrity and contempt for luxury; but the remark is elsewhere ascribed to another paragon of ancient Roman virtue, Manius Curius Dentatus.

37. *interrupting some comedy:* when More was in Morton's household, 'though young of years, yet would he at Christmas tide suddenly sometimes step in among the players, and never studying for the matter, make a part of his own there presently among them, which made the lookers on more sport than all the players beside.' (Roper, *Life*, p. 5.)

38. *scene in the Octavia:* lines 440–588, where Seneca is trying to persuade Nero to be a good ruler instead of a bloody tyrant.

39. *everything He ... housetops:* Luke, xii, 3: 'that which ye have spoken in the ear in closets shall be proclaimed upon the housetops'.

40. *Micio in Terence: Adelphoe*, 146–7.

41. *image in Plato:* More's simile is a very free paraphrase of *Republic*, VI, 496d–e.

42. *for a city:* Megalopolis in Arcadia, founded about 370 B.C.

BOOK TWO

1. *sort of crescent:* but the tips of a crescent moon do not come close enough together. It is better imagined in the shape of the crescent on the Turkish flag, where the points do practically meet to form a circle, and the star can serve as the rock in the harbour-mouth.

2. *extraordinary method:* according to Pliny (*Natural History*, X, 54), the Egyptians used the heat of dung-heaps for artificial incubation. It seems quite plausible that Utopian chicks should become fixated on a human being. Dr K. D. Lorenz describes a similar experience with a young jackdaw: 'Just as the quills of its primary feathers became hard and ready for flight, my young bird suddenly developed a really childlike affection for my person. It refused to remain by itself for a second, flew after me from one room to another and called in desperation if ever I was forced to leave it alone.' (*King Solomon's Ring,* London, 1961, p. 130.)

3. *Mayor:* the original word is *princeps* (chief, leader, or in late Latin, prince). Robinson translated it as 'prince', and so started a long series of references by critics to the 'king' of Utopia; but it is clear from the text that the *princeps* is merely the chief magistrate of a town. Utopia is a republic, not a monarchy.

4. *Barzanes:* the Utopian language is 'like Persian' (p. 100) and this name has Persian associations. It was probably suggested to More by *Mithrobarzanes,* the name of Menippus's guide to the Underworld in Lucian's *Menippus* (which More translated into Latin). Mithrobarzanes is there described as 'a very wise and incredibly learned Chaldaean, with white hair and a most impressive beard'. It is appropriate that the title of a Utopian Mayor should have such associations of age, wisdom, learning, and religion (*Mythras* is the Utopian word for 'God').

5. *but we could . . . scarcity-value:* this part of the sentence was added in the 1518 text.

6. *better than a sheep:* the joke is borrowed from Lucian (*Demonax,* 41).

7. *Introduction to Logic:* the *Summulae Logicales* of Petrus Juliani or Hispanus, who was Pope 1276–7. It is referred to here as the *Parva Logicalia* (Little Logic), its usual nickname – doubtless, as More had

written in a letter of 21 October 1515, because there was little logic in it. (*Correspondence of Sir Thomas More*, Princeton, 1947, p. 38.)

8. *Second Intentions:* 'First Intentions' are 'primary conceptions of things, formed by the first or direct application of the mind to the things themselves, e.g. the concepts of *a tree, an oak*'. '*Second Intentions*' are 'secondary conceptions formed by the application of thought to First Intentions in their relations to each other, e.g. the concepts of *genus, species, variety, property, accident, difference, identity*'. (N.E.D.)

9. *Universal, MAN*: an allusion to the famous medieval controversy between Realists (who believed that Universals had a real existence apart from individual things) and Nominalists (who thought that Universals were merely *names*). The joke is adapted from Lucian's satire on Plato's Ideas. (Penguin Classics Lucian, pp. 157–8.)

10. *experts in astronomy:* the wording of the original ('experts in the course of the stars and the motion of the celestial spheres') shows that the Utopians subscribe to the Ptolemaic system, according to which the earth is encircled by a number of crystal shells, called 'spheres', revolving at different speeds, and carrying the planets, etc., with them.

11. *following one's natural impulses:* literally, 'to live according to nature', which is the Stoic definition of virtue; but the Utopians' emphasis on pleasure makes them more like the people described by Vespucci, who 'live according to nature, and may be called Epicureans rather than Stoics'. (*New World.*)

12. *either way:* 'The staff of the Pall Mall Safe Deposit in the Haymarket, which is due for demolition, anticipate being left with getting on for 200 unclaimed safe deposits to open, in spite of all the efforts they will be making to trace the owners. Some of them will be dead ... Many will just have forgotten.' (*New Statesman*, 20.7.1962.)

13. *far more sparingly:* I have translated the reading of the first edition, *multo magis conservant* (they preserve or spare far more). The 1518 reading, *multo magis conferunt* (they confer much more benefit) seems tautological, in view of the previous *utiliores* (more or relatively useful).

14. *hunger:* the original text has the participle, *esurientem* (being hungry), but the word is corrected to the noun, *esuriem* (hunger) in the collected Latin Works (1565).

15. *rubbing and scratching:* the argument is taken from Plato's *Gorgias*, 494, c.

16. *some traces of Greek:* practically all the proper names are of Greek derivation (see Introduction, p. 8, and Glossary).

17. *a monkey:* More was very fond of animals, and kept several,

including a monkey, a fox, a beaver, and a weasel, at his home in Chelsea.

18. *Lascaris:* the Greek grammar of Constantine Lascaris was published at Milan in 1476, under the title of *Erotemata* (Questions).

19. *Theodorus:* i.e. Theodorus Gaza, whose four-volume Greek grammar was published in 1495.

20. *Hesychius:* an Alexandrian scholar who probably lived in the fifth century A.D., and whose Greek Lexicon was printed at Venice in 1514.

21. *Dioscorides:* I cannot trace anyone of this name who wrote a dictionary. Perhaps the reference is to Dioscorides (or Dioscurides) the Younger, who lived during the reign of Hadrian (A.D. 117–38) and compiled a glossary to the works of Hippocrates, which Hesychius later incorporated in his Lexicon.

22. *Herodianus* (about A.D. 165–250) wrote a history of the Roman Emperors from the death of Marcus Aurelius (A.D. 180) to A.D. 238 which was very popular during the Renaissance.

23. *Galen's Handbook:* the original has 'Galen's *Microtechne* (little art)', the medieval name for his *Art of Medicine,* as opposed to his *Megalotechnum* (big art), i.e. *Therapeutic Method* in fourteen books.

24. *Aldus:* Aldo Manuzio, the famous Venetian printer, had very recently died (April 1515).

25. *non-combatant prisoners-of-war:* in the ancient world, that is what slaves usually were. It is not quite clear whether *combatant* P.O.W.'s were ever enslaved in Utopia. The original words are: *Pro servis neque bello captos habent, nisi ab ipsis gesto* (as slaves they do not have people captured in war, unless it was waged by themselves). This may mean either that they enslave everyone caught fighting on the battlefield, or else that they only enslave those *responsible* for waging the war, i.e. supporters of war policies.

26. *when . . . a horse:* the argument, including the horse image, is taken from a passage in Horace (*Satires,* 1, ii, 83–105) which shows why fornication is better than adultery. For one thing, with a prostitute you can at least see what you are getting, whereas married women are always over-dressed. In *A Sermon against Adultery* Pope turned this point rather unkindly against Lady Mary Wortley Montagu:

> A lady's face is all you see undress'd
> (For none but Lady M . . . shows the rest) . . . (124–5)

27. *old age . . . itself:* possibly suggested by Terence (*Phormio,* 575).

28. *mentally deficient:* it seems to me that in this context (immediately before a reference to physical deformity) *moriones* (fools) means

people of sub-normal intelligence: hence the importance of seeing that they are looked after properly. Certainly many 'Fools' came into this category: 'The court-fool ... causes amusement not merely by absurd gluttony, merry gossip, or knavish tricks, but by mental deficiencies or physical deformities which deprive him both of rights and responsibilities, and put him in the paradoxical position of virtual outlawry combined with utter dependence on the support of the social group to which he belongs' (Enid Welsford, *The Fool*, London, 1935, p. 55). More's own 'fool', Henry Patenson, however, seems to have been far from unintelligent. When More was in the Tower, for refusing to take the oath required by the Act of Succession, Master Harry became exasperated and asked: 'Why, what aileth him that he will not swear? Wherefore should he stick to swear? I have sworn the oath myself.' (*English Works*, 1557, p. 1441 G).

29. *that he carries ... carries:* the Latin words (*gestatus, praelatus*) could mean that these symbols are carried by attendants; but, since the whole emphasis is on non-formality, I suspect that the Mayors and Bishops do the carrying (though they must, in practice, find it rather difficult to perform their duties single-handed).

30. *can't be bribed:* unlike Bacon, one of his successors in the office of Lord Chancellor, More never accepted a bribe, and skilfully walked the tightrope between discourtesy and corruption, when offered presents by interested parties. One gave him a gilt cup, which he promptly returned, after drinking the donor's health in it; another brought him a 'New Year's gift', which was again a gilt cup: More liked the design, and kept it – but reciprocated with a more valuable cup of his own.

31. *the Popes:* the satirical target is probably Pope Julius II (1443–1513). For a specimen of his diplomatic methods one may quote his dealings with France and Venice. In 1508 he joined Louis XII in the League of Cambrai against Venice. Having forced the Venetians, with French support, into submission in 1509, he then formed the Holy League in 1510, by which he allied himself with Venice against France.

32. *quite subhuman:* there is an untranslatable pun on *bellum* (war) and *belluinam* (beastly).

33. *the Venalians:* the originals of this national portrait are probably the Swiss, who regularly fought in many of the armies of Europe during the period. Between 1465 and 1715 over a million Swiss soldiers served in France alone.

34. *fight like heroes:* literally, 'and often extreme necessity is turned into courage' (*et saepe extrema necessitas in virtutem vertitur*). I have

reluctantly avoided the proverbial phrase, 'make a virtue of necessity', because *virtue* has now ceased to mean 'manhood, courage', and the whole expression has taken on a pejorative implication (taking credit for doing what one is forced to do), which seems out of place in the context.

35. *the frontier:* the first part of the sentence seems to refer to Utopian territory overseas. 'On their own soil' is literally 'on their *lands*' (*in suis terris*).

36. *Mythras,* or Mithras (the normal spelling) was the Persian god of light. Mithraism had some resemblances to Christianity (e.g. its rites included baptism, and the ritual drinking of a mixture of flour and water), and was widespread among members of the Roman army. Temples of Mithras have been found in Northumberland, at York, and very recently in London.

37. *prescribed ... way of life:* literally 'a communal living of his people pleased Christ' (*Christo communem suorum victum placuisse*), but *placeo* is regularly used to express a regulation or decision made by a ruler or government, so I do not think the word *prescribed* is too strong. There is, of course, no recorded statement by Jesus expressing approval of communism, but His answer to the man who 'had great possessions' (Mark, x, 21) implies that His disciples did not retain any private property; and it is clear from Acts, ii, 44-5, and iv, 32, that the early Church was organized on communist lines.

38. *truly Christian communities:* a marginal note explains that this means monasteries and convents.

39. *religious toleration:* although the worst charges of cruelty to heretics during his Chancellorship have not been substantiated, there seems to be no doubt that More sentenced some people to death (which meant burning alive) for heresy. While writing in his own defence, two years before he died, he admitted, without any sign of embarrassment, that he had made a remark about the Protestant, John Frith, which implies that Christ is personally responsible for burning heretics: '. . . I would some good friend of his should show him, that I fear me sore that *Christ will kindle a fire of faggots for him,* and make him therein sweat the blood out of his body here . . .' (*Apology*, London, 1930, p. 137; my italics). The contradiction between More's attitude to heretics and this passage in *Utopia* is not quite so sharp as it seems at first. For one thing, Utopian toleration applies only in a limited degree to atheists; for another, preaching religious beliefs in such a way as to cause a disturbance of the peace is a prosecutable offence – and More evidently regarded heretics as subverters of civilized society. But a certain inconsistency remains, and no humane person who otherwise admires More can help being

horrified to find him taking such a very un-Utopian line in real life.

40. *cheerful and optimistic mood:* More's famous jokes on the scaffold show how successfully he lived up to this ideal: 'Where, going up the scaffold, which was so weak that it was ready to fall, he said merrily to Master Lieutenant: "I pray you, Master Lieutenant, see me safe up, and for my coming down let me shift for myself" . . . he kneeled down, and, after his prayers said, turned to the executioner, and with a cheerful countenance spake thus to him: "Pluck up thy spirits, man, and be not afraid to do thine office; my neck is very short; take heed therefore thou strike not awry, for saving of thine honesty."' (Roper, *Life*, pp. 102–3.)

41. *Cowparsons:* the etymological basis of this 'equivalent' is explained in the Glossary. I think its satirical effect may be justified by the tone of the language in which they are described on page 122 (e.g. the comic associations of *inhiant,* which I have translated 'yearn for', but which literally means, 'to stare at with one's mouth open'), and also by the general argument of the passage: the point is that the behaviour of these people is from a commonsense, if not from a religious point of view, ridiculous. Of course More went in for similar ascetic practices himself; but he was quite capable of seeing his own actions in a humorous light.

The word translated 'Lay Brethren' is *religiosi* (religious people, or, in Christian authors, members of religious orders).

42. *priests . . . marry:* in *A Dialogue concerning Heresies* (1528) More discusses and rejects the suggestion that priests should be allowed to marry:

In the old law given to Moses, the priests of the temple for the time of their ministration forbare their own house and the company of their wives . . . So that chastity was thought both to God and man a thing meet and convenient for priests, among them which most magnified carnal generation. And then how much more specially now to the priests of Christ, which was both born [of] a virgin, and lived and died a virgin Himself, and exhorted all His to the same. Whose counsel in that point, since some be content to follow, and some to live otherwise, what way were, I say, more meetly than to take into Christ's temple to serve about the sacrament only such as be of that sort that are content and minded to live after the cleanness of Christ's holy counsel?

(*English Works,* 1557, p. 232 G–H.)

His reaction to Luther's marriage was to call him 'an open incestuous lecher'. (*English Works,* p. 247H.)

43. *woman . . . priest:* later in the same dialogue More deals with Luther's statement that any man or woman is qualified to hear confession and give absolution:

Marry, sir, quoth your friend, this were an easy way for one thing. For the sorest thing that I find in confession is that when I see many confessors at a pardon, yet can I scant like one of them so well upon the sight, that I would tell any such tales to once in seven year, and [i.e. if] I might choose. But now, if I might after Luther's way be confessed to a fair woman, I would not let to be confessed weekly.

Ye would, quoth I, peradventure tell her a tale that ye would not tell every man . . .

Yes, yes, quoth I, a woman can keep a counsel well enough. For though she tell a gossip, she telleth it but in counsel [i.e. in confidence] yet, nor her gossip to her gossip neither, and so when all the gossips in the town know it, yet it is but counsel still.

(*English Works*, p. 249 c–d; 250 c.)

In the *Confutation of Tyndale's Answer* (1532) More replies to Tyndale's assertion that women 'may and ought to minister not only baptism but all other sacraments also in time of need'; his final argument is based, not on reason, but on revelation (to which the Utopians, of course, have no access):

Now if Tyndale ask me why a woman may christen and not consecrate since both are sacraments, I can answer him the common answer that though both be necessary, yet both be not like great nor like necessary. . . . But as for my part, I will give him none answer to the question other than the ordinance of God's Spirit, which I see that God hath taught His Church; and else would He not suffer them to believe that it were well done, whereof no man is bound to give a precise cause. But it were overmuch boldness to think that we could precisely tell the cause of everything that it pleaseth God to devise . . .

(*English Works*, p. 462 f–g.)

44. *cream . . . society:* the original words, *sacerdotibus . . . uxores sunt popularium selectissimae* (priests' wives are the most select members of the population) may mean either that priests' wives are highly respected members of society (a paradox in More's day), or that priests are themselves so highly respected that they have the pick of all the females in the country, when they are looking for wives. I have chosen the first interpretation, as being the slightly more natural, and less Rabelaisian way of taking the Latin.

45. *feathers:* in Plato's *Phaedrus* (251a–c), when an unworldly-minded person sees 'a god-like face', he is reminded of heavenly beauty, and his soul begins to sprout the wings that it lost when it became imprisoned in an earthly body. In Vespucci's *Four Voyages* (mentioned by Peter Gilles on page 38), some natives of the New World are described, whose greatest treasures are multicoloured bird's-feathers. (*Cosmographiae Introductio*, St Dié, 1507, p. 53.) These two

passages may have combined to suggest the character of Utopian vestments.

46. *a republic:* there were not many states besides Venice which called themselves republics in More's day; but I was compelled to use the word, which is appropriate enough nowadays, in order to retain the verbal link between *respublica* (public thing, property, or interest) and *publicum commodum* (public advantage or profit).

47. *producing luxury goods:* this is a legitimate method of translating *adulatores* (flatterers), if I am right in seeing a reference to Plato's *Gorgias* (463a–b), where rhetoric, sophistry, cookery, and beauty treatment are categorized as forms of *kolakeia* (flattery), because they give people what they want, instead of what is good for them.

48. *injustice . . . justice:* 'This passage clearly refers to the legislation of recent parliaments, completed in the parliament of 1515, which re-enacted the old statutes against labourers while removing clauses unfavourable to employers.' (R. Ames, *Citizen Thomas More and his Utopia,* Princeton, 1949, p. 128.)

49. *black magic:* it seems odd that after pouring scorn on fortune-telling, astrology, and similar superstitions (pp. 90, 121–2), Nonsenso should list black magic as a serious crime; but if *veneficia* is given its primary meaning of 'poisonings', it partially duplicates the preceding 'murders'.

50. *sucking-fish:* the remora, which was then thought capable of retarding the movement of a ship.

51. *in Europe:* literally 'in our states' (*in nostris civitatibus*).

APPENDIX

More's Attitude to Communism

Certain passages in More's other works may be thought to suggest that his praise of communism in *Utopia* should not be taken seriously. In his *In Lutherum* (1523) More sets out to refute Luther's 'very silly statement'

> that the law of the Gospel would be sufficient by itself, and human laws would serve no useful purpose, if magistrates were good, and the Faith were preached truly. As if the best magistrates in the world could bring it about that *all Christian people* wanted to live on a communist system, or that wicked people did not want to steal; or as if any preaching of the Faith could ensure that there were no wicked people anywhere!
>
> If the law of the Gospel forbids theft, then certainly human law, which punishes theft, does serve some useful purpose, and Christians are bound to obey human law, which is the sole origin of the distribution of property, and without which theft could not exist.
>
> But if he claims to base his argument on the theory that we should do better to dispense with the law which creates property, and to live in a sort of natural communism, he does not strengthen his case, *even if one were to grant him the truth of that theory*; for even if one could live under a communist system with far fewer laws, one still could not live without any laws whatever. Certain regulations would still have to be made for compulsory work, and laws would be needed to suppress crimes, which would still cause trouble even in a life like that.
>
> Now, granted that, even if the Faith were preached with that absolute truthfulness that characterized the preaching of the Apostles, and even if the best possible magistrates were everywhere in control of Christian people, *property might still remain*, and many wicked individuals would remain, he cannot deny that human law obliges Christians not to grab anything that the law has allocated to someone else, and that human law does serve a useful purpose in punishing anyone who commits theft.
>
> (Opera, 1565, p. 80, verso; my italics.)

One might conceivably deduce from the second paragraph that communism is wrong, because it makes nonsense of the Commandment incorporated in the Gospel (Matthew xix, 18): 'Thou shalt not steal'; but that, of course, is not what the passage is getting at. Its function is to prove that, whether or not you adopt a communist system, human laws are necessary. If you live in a society based on private property, human laws are needed to establish what belongs to whom, and so to define and prevent theft. If you live in a communist society, where theft is logically impossible, you still need laws to suppress other forms of crime, and to regulate compulsory work. Nothing is said explicitly against communism; and the three groups of words that I have italicized imply, at least, a tolerant attitude towards it. The first suggests that *some* Christians, though not all, will want to live on a communist system; the second, that communist theory is not a totally unacceptable hypothesis; and the third, that under ideal conditions private property would not necessarily exist, though wicked people would.

There is another reference to communism in the *Confutation of Tyndale's Answer* (1532–3):

And so ye may see that Tyndale affirmeth now not only those abominable heresies he taught before, but all those also the Anabaptists have added unto them since. And so now be the true church with him, and agree with Scripture and with the law of God, all those that say the baptizing of children is void, and they that say there ought to be no rulers at all in Christendom, neither spiritual nor temporal, and that no man should have anything proper of his own, but that all lands and all goods ought *by God's law* to be all men's in common, and that all women ought to be common to all men, as well the next of kin as the farthest stranger, and every man husband to every woman, and every woman wife unto every man, and then finally that our blessed Saviour Christ was but only man and not God at all.

(*English Works*, 1557, p. 656 G–H; my italics.)

Here communism seems, at first sight, to be classed as an 'abominable heresy'; but the phrase which I have italicized shows that the heresy consists in maintaining that communism is obligatory on religious grounds. In the rhetorical structure of the passage, the allusion to common ownership of lands and goods serves mainly, I suspect, to introduce the ultimate abomination of sexual promiscuity and incest; certainly More's immediate purpose is not to attack communism, but to ridicule Tyndale's statement:

As they which depart from the faith of the true church are heretics, even so they that depart from the church of heretics and false feigned faith of hypocrites, are the true church.

(*English Works*, 1557, p. 655 A–B.)

If, says More, unorthodoxy is the only qualification for membership of Tyndale's 'true church', it must include a surprising variety of doctrines.

Finally, in *A Dialogue of Comfort against Tribulation* (1534), More wrote as follows:

But cousin, men of substance must there be, for else shall you have more beggars ... than there be, and no man left to relieve another. For this I think in my mind a very sure conclusion, that if all the money that is in this country were tomorrow next brought together out of every man's hand, and laid all upon one heap, and then divided out unto every man alike, it would be on the morrow after, worse than it was the day before. For I suppose when it were all equally thus divided among all, the best should be left little better then, than almost a beggar is now. And yet he that was a beggar before, all that [i.e. although] he shall be the richer for that he should thereby receive, shall not make him much above a beggar still, but many one of the rich men, if their riches stood but in movable substance shall be safe enough from riches haply for all their life after.

Men cannot, you wot well, live here *in this world,* but if some one man provide a mean of living for some other many. Every man cannot have a ship of his own, nor every man be a merchant without a stock – and these things you wot well needs must be had – nor every man cannot have a plough by himself. And who might live by the taylor's craft, if no man were able to put a gown to make? Who by the masonry, or who could live a carpenter, if no man were able to build neither church nor house? Who should be the makers of any manner cloth, if there lacked men of substance to set sundry sorts a-work? Some man that hath not two ducats in his house, were better forbear them both and leave himself not a farthing but utterly lose all his own, than that some rich man by whom he is weekly set a-work, should of his money lose the one half. For there were himself like to lack work. For surely the rich man's substance is the well-spring of the poor man's living.

(*English Works,* 1557, p. 1207 H–1208 C; my italics.)

This has been described as 'a most emphatic contradiction of the very principle of communism'. (H. W. Donner, *Introduction to Utopia,* 1945, p. 66.) It is really nothing of the kind. The 'cousin' (who is actually a nephew) has raised a moral and religious problem:

I cannot well perceive (*the world being such as it is,* and so many poor people therein) how any man may be rich and keep him rich without danger of damnation therefore.

(*English Works,* 1557, p. 1204 G; my italics.)

His uncle replies that, in spite of the Gospel injunction: 'Give to every man that asketh of thee' (Luke, vi, 30), it is not a Christian's duty to give away *all* his property in alms, because 'in this world', i.e. under the present system, rich men play an essential part in the economic structure of society. Neither speaker for a moment envisages a communist system, in which the role of employer would, of course, be taken over by the community itself.

I have yet to see any conclusive evidence that More did not mean what he said about communism in *Utopia.*

GLOSSARY

AIRCASTLE: *Amaurotum,* from *amauros* (dim, faint, shadowy), the adjective applied by Homer to the vision of Athene which appears to Penelope in a dream. (*Odyssey,* IV, 824, 835.) Presumably the name means 'dream-town'.

BENCHEATER: *Traniborus,* possibly from *thranos* (bench) and *bora* (food). If so, the name may have been suggested by memories of Lincoln's Inn, where More's grandfather and father had both held the post of butler, and he himself had been a Reader; where communal meals were eaten by members sitting on benches; and where Senior Members were known as Benchers.

BLINDLANDERS: *Alaopolitae,* from *alaos* (blind) and *polites* (citizen).

CLOUDIANS: *Nephelogetae,* from *nephele* (cloud).

COWPARSONS: *Buthrescae,* from *threskos* (religious, or superstitious), with the prefix *bou-*, from *bous* (cow, bull, ox), used in compounds to indicate 'huge, monstrous' (e.g. *boukoruza,* a violent cold in the head), rather like the prefixes *cow-* and *horse-* in English. So the name seems to imply exaggerated piety.

DISTRICT CONTROLLER: *Phylarchus,* from *phule* (tribe, especially one of the tribes into which the Athenian population was divided) and *archos* (chief, ruler).

DOGDATES: *Cynemerni,* apparently from *kuon, kunos* (dog) and *hemera* (day). In ancient Greece, on the night before the new moon, food was placed outside people's houses as an offering to Hecate. There are three possible links between this custom and dogs: in Theocritus (II, 35–6) the barking of dogs indicates the approach of Hecate; the goddess herself was usually accompanied by hellhounds; and the appearance of a plate of food on every doorstep would certainly make the occasion a sort of benefit night for dogs.

FLATULENTINE: *Anemolius,* from *anemos* (wind, internal as well as external). See WINDBAG.

HAPPILAND: *Macarenses,* from *makar* (happy).

LIETALK: *Senatus Mentiranus,* presumably from *mentiri* (lie), as though the *-ment* in *Parliament* were derived from this verb. More had learnt from experience that Parliament was a place where it was dangerous to speak the truth (see p. 139, note 35). Later he evidently decided that it was confusing to call his ideal Utopian Parliament by a name which satirized the real English one; so in the 1518 edition he replaced *Mentiranus* by *Amauroticus* (at Aircastle).

NOLANDIA: *Achoriorum populus,* the people of the *achorii,* from *a-* (not and *chora* (country).

NONSENSO: *Hythlodaeus,* from *hythlos* (nonsense) and *daio* (distribute).

NOPEOPLE: *Ademus,* from *a-* (not) and *demos* (people).

NOWATER: *Anydrus,* from *a-* (not) and *hudor* (water).

SANSCULOTTIA: *Abraxa.* My 'equivalent' is based on a rash conjecture that the word is derived from *a-* (not) and *brakae* (breeches). Some commentators connect Abraxa with Abraxas, a mystic term invented by Basilides, a Gnostic philosopher of the second century A.D., to signify the supreme deity, whose 365 emanations created and controlled 365 different heavens (the ancient Greeks employed letters as numbers, and the numerical value of the letters in *Abraxas* is 365). Personally I do not think there is any reference to Abraxas here. If there were, why should More have omitted the final *s,* thus reducing the figure to a mere 165 ? Besides, it is clear from the context that, far from being a sort of 'heaven', Abraxa was an extremely backward country inhabited by 'a pack of ignorant savages'. It seems more reasonable to assume that the name is formed on the same principle as *Achorii, Ademos,* and *Anydrus,* and that the initial *a-* indicates a negative.

SENIOR DISTRICT CONTROLLER: *Protophylarchus,* from *protos* (first), *phule* (tribe), and *archos* (ruler).

STY: see STYWARD.

STYWARD: *Syphograntus,* possibly from *supheos* (pig-sty) and *krantor* (ruler). Like *Traniborus,* this name may have some connexion with Lincoln's Inn, where More's grandfather was not only butler but also steward (which was sometimes spelt *styward*). I have used the word *Sty* to translate *Syphograntia,* the group of households administered by a Syphogrant.

TALLSTORIA: the country of the *Polyleritae,* from *polus* (much) and *leros* (nonsense).

TOMMY ROT: *Tricius Apinatus,* from Trica and Apina, two small towns in Apulia. Because of their poverty and insignificance, both names came to be used in the plural, either singly or together, to signify 'trifles, worthless stuff, nonsense' (e.g. in Martial, XIV, i, 7).

TURNDATES: *Trapemerni,* from *trap-,* aorist stem of *trepo* (turn, change) and *hemera* (day). The name seems to mean the day on which one changes from the old month to the new.

VENALIANS: *Zapoletae,* from *za-* (an intensifying prefix) and *poleo* (sell) or *poletes* (seller).

WINDBAG: *Anemolius,* from *anemos* (wind). See FLATULENTINE.

hansenbs@witcc.com

Kimberly mickelson @
hotmail.com

READ MORE IN PENGUIN

In every corner of the world, on every subject under the sun, Penguin represents quality and variety – the very best in publishing today.

For complete information about books available from Penguin – including Puffins, Penguin Classics and Arkana – and how to order them, write to us at the appropriate address below. Please note that for copyright reasons the selection of books varies from country to country.

In the United Kingdom: Please write to *Dept. EP, Penguin Books Ltd, Bath Road, Harmondsworth, West Drayton, Middlesex UB7 ODA*

In the United States: Please write to *Consumer Sales, Penguin USA, P.O. Box 999, Dept. 17109, Bergenfield, New Jersey 07621-0120*. VISA and MasterCard holders call 1-800-253-6476 to order Penguin titles

In Canada: Please write to *Penguin Books Canada Ltd, 10 Alcorn Avenue, Suite 300, Toronto, Ontario M4V 3B2*

In Australia: Please write to *Penguin Books Australia Ltd, P.O. Box 257, Ringwood, Victoria 3134*

In New Zealand: Please write to *Penguin Books (NZ) Ltd, Private Bag 102902, North Shore Mail Centre, Auckland 10*

In India: Please write to *Penguin Books India Pvt Ltd, 706 Eros Apartments, 56 Nehru Place, New Delhi 110 019*

In the Netherlands: Please write to *Penguin Books Netherlands bv, Postbus 3507, NL-1001 AH Amsterdam*

In Germany: Please write to *Penguin Books Deutschland GmbH, Metzlerstrasse 26, 60594 Frankfurt am Main*

In Spain: Please write to *Penguin Books S. A., Bravo Murillo 19, 1° B, 28015 Madrid*

In Italy: Please write to *Penguin Italia s.r.l., Via Felice Casati 20, I–20124 Milano*

In France: Please write to *Penguin France S. A., 17 rue Lejeune, F–31000 Toulouse*

In Japan: Please write to *Penguin Books Japan, Ishikiribashi Building, 2–5–4, Suido, Bunkyo-ku, Tokyo 112*

In South Africa: Please write to *Longman Penguin Southern Africa (Pty) Ltd, Private Bag X08, Bertsham 2013*

PENGUIN AUDIOBOOKS

A Quality of Writing That Speaks for Itself

Penguin Books has always led the field in quality publishing. Now you can listen at leisure to your favourite books, read to you by familiar voices from radio, stage and screen. Penguin Audiobooks are produced to an excellent standard, and abridgements are always faithful to the original texts. From thrillers to classic literature, biography to humour, with a wealth of titles in between, Penguin Audiobooks offer you quality, entertainment and the chance to rediscover the pleasure of listening.

You can order Penguin Audiobooks through Penguin Direct by telephoning (0181) 899 4036. The lines are open 24 hours every day. Ask for Penguin Direct, quoting your credit card details.

A selection of Penguin Audiobooks, published or forthcoming:

Little Women by Louisa May Alcott, read by Kate Harper

Emma by Jane Austen, read by Fiona Shaw

Pride and Prejudice by Jane Austen, read by Geraldine McEwan

Beowulf translated by Michael Alexander, read by David Rintoul

Agnes Grey by Anne Brontë, read by Juliet Stevenson

Jane Eyre by Charlotte Brontë, read by Juliet Stevenson

The Professor by Charlotte Brontë, read by Juliet Stevenson

Wuthering Heights by Emily Brontë, read by Juliet Stevenson

The Woman in White by Wilkie Collins, read by Nigel Anthony and Susan Jameson

Nostromo by Joseph Conrad, read by Michael Pennington

Tales from the Thousand and One Nights, read by Souad Faress and Raad Rawi

Robinson Crusoe by Daniel Defoe, read by Tom Baker

David Copperfield by Charles Dickens, read by Nathaniel Parker

The Pickwick Papers by Charles Dickens, read by Dinsdale Landen

Bleak House by Charles Dickens, read by Beatie Edney and Ronald Pickup

Anna Karenina by Fyodor Dostoyevsky, read by Juliet Stevenson

PENGUIN AUDIOBOOKS

Crime and Punishment by Fyodor Dostoyevsky, read by Alex Jennings

Middlemarch by George Eliot, read by Harriet Walter

Silas Marner by George Eliot, read by Tim Pigott-Smith

The Great Gatsby by F. Scott Fitzgerald, read by Marcus D'Amico

Madame Bovary by Gustave Flaubert, read by Claire Bloom

Jude the Obscure by Thomas Hardy, read by Samuel West

The Return of the Native by Thomas Hardy, read by Steven Pacey

Tess of the D'Urbervilles by Thomas Hardy, read by Eleanor Bron

The Iliad by Homer, read by Derek Jacobi

Dubliners by James Joyce, read by Gerard McSorley

The Dead and Other Stories by James Joyce, read by Gerard McSorley

On the Road by Jack Kerouac, read by David Carradine

Sons and Lovers by D. H. Lawrence, read by Paul Copley

The Fall of the House of Usher by Edgar Allan Poe, read by Andrew Sachs

Wide Sargasso Sea by Jean Rhys, read by Jane Lapotaire and Michael Kitchen

The Little Prince by Antoine de Saint-Exupéry, read by Michael Maloney

Frankenstein by Mary Shelley, read by Richard Pasco

Of Mice and Men by John Steinbeck, read by Gary Sinise

Travels with Charley by John Steinbeck, read by Gary Sinise

The Pearl by John Steinbeck, read by Hector Elizondo

Dr Jekyll and Mr Hyde by Robert Louis Stevenson, read by Jonathan Hyde

Kidnapped by Robert Louis Stevenson, read by Robbie Coltrane

The Age of Innocence by Edith Wharton, read by Kerry Shale

The Buccaneers by Edith Wharton, read by Dana Ivey

Mrs Dalloway by Virginia Woolf, read by Eileen Atkins

READ MORE IN PENGUIN

A CHOICE OF CLASSICS

St Anselm	**The Prayers and Meditations**
St Augustine	**The Confessions**
Bede	**Ecclesiastical History of the English People**
Geoffrey Chaucer	**The Canterbury Tales**
	Love Visions
	Troilus and Criseyde
Marie de France	**The Lais of Marie de France**
Jean Froissart	**The Chronicles**
Geoffrey of Monmouth	**The History of the Kings of Britain**
Gerald of Wales	**History and Topography of Ireland**
	The Journey through Wales and **The Description of Wales**
Gregory of Tours	**The History of the Franks**
Robert Henryson	**The Testament of Cresseid and Other Poems**
Walter Hilton	**The Ladder of Perfection**
Julian of Norwich	**Revelations of Divine Love**
Thomas à Kempis	**The Imitation of Christ**
William Langland	**Piers the Ploughman**
Sir John Mandeville	**The Travels of Sir John Mandeville**
Marguerite de Navarre	**The Heptameron**
Christine de Pisan	**The Treasure of the City of Ladies**
Chrétien de Troyes	**Arthurian Romances**
Marco Polo	**The Travels**
Richard Rolle	**The Fire of Love**
François Villon	**Selected Poems**